God
in Our
Relationships

Spirituality between People from the Teachings of Martin Buber

Rabbi Dennis S. Ross

For People of All Faiths, All Backgrounds
JEWISH LIGHTS Publishing
Woodstock, Vermont

God in Our Relationships:
Spirituality between People from the Teachings of Martin Buber

© 2003 by Dennis S. Ross

Library of Congress Cataloging-in-Publication Data
Ross, Dennis S. (Dennis Sidney), 1953–
God in our relationships : spirituality between people from the teachings of Martin Buber / Dennis S. Ross.
         p. cm.
Includes bibliographical references and index.
ISBN 1-58023-147-0 (pbk.)
1. Spiritual life—Judaism. 2. Interpersonal relations—Religious aspects—Judaism. 3. Ross, Dennis S. (Dennis Sidney), 1953–
4. Relationism. 5. Buber, Martin, 1878–1965. Ich und du. I. Title.
BM723 .R57 2003
296.7—dc21

2002153387

10 9 8 7 6 5 4 3 2 1

Manufactured in the United States of America

For People of All Faiths, All Backgrounds
Published by Jewish Lights Publishing
A Division of LongHill Partners, Inc.
Sunset Farm Offices, Route 4, P.O. Box 237
Woodstock, VT 05091
Tel: (802) 457-4000   Fax: (802) 457-4004
www.jewishlights.com

To Debbie:
You live these words.

Contents

Part Three
I-Thou: When One Voice Lifts Another

Part Four
I-Thou on the Narrow Ridge

Part Five
Eternal Thou: A Leap of Faith

I swear that one & one are three:
I see it always so
when lovers kiss
& friends embrace.

—*Chaim Stern,* Gates of Forgiveness

PREFACE

To [people] the world is twofold ...[1]

This book explores the spirituality between people, based on the teachings of Martin Buber. Using the terminology from Buber's landmark book, *I and Thou*, I discuss new ways to understand the various degrees of human relationships—and more.

Martin Buber said that he was not a philosopher but an ordinary person who saw something interesting through a window and called others forward to share his observation. In *God in Our Relationships*, I invite you to peer through the window of my life for a view of the landscape I see.

I present a lattice structure, composed of Buber's work, particularly *I and Thou*, as well as the Hasidic stories Buber loved; the Jewish tradition; the science of human behavior; and two decades of experience as a congregational rabbi. I organize and retell what these years have taught me, what I have learned from books and from people.

From books, I quote directly or try to recast faithfully. When it comes to the lessons I learned from people, I have heavily disguised their personal narratives in order to honor their privacy. Even under this heavy cloak of confidentiality, the life of the clergyman or clergywoman speaks to everyone.

In the course of a single day, most people, like me, are busy and empty, hurrying and helping, elated and in distress. We confront obstacles we neither recognize nor understand. All the while, we wander in and out of relationships as a lost traveler sojourns in the wilderness.

Alone in the desert, Jacob of the Bible took a rock for a night's pillow and suddenly woke in the dark, awestruck at the sight of a procession of angels leaving and returning to the heavens. Unbeknownst to Jacob, an ordinary, desolate patch of desert was a divine abode! A shocked Jacob declared, "God is here and I did not even notice!"[2]

Like Jacob, we can go through a day or a lifetime as sleepwalkers while awake, tossing and turning on pillows that are as hard as appointment books, wandering a paved spiritual wilderness from bank window to house of worship to hospital bedside. If we are fortunate to happen upon a vision of the Divine—in the chance chat with a semi-stranger or a lingering conversation with a good friend—we suddenly awaken to the spirituality between people that Martin Buber called the *I-Thou* relationship.

About the Translations

Unless otherwise noted, all translations from Hebrew are mine.

ACKNOWLEDGMENTS

The soulful responses of friends and colleagues brought vitality and color to *God in Our Relationships*. These readers spoke to me as Martin Buber taught us to address one another—with an openness and fullness that enlivened and enriched each page:

Rabbinic mentors and colleagues Rabbi Eugene Borowitz; Professor Carol Ochs; Rabbi Jessica Spitalnic; Rabbi Jack Stern; and, of blessed memory, Rabbi Chaim Stern.

Christian clergy Rev. Joel Huntington, Rev. Robert Kyte, Major Thomas Perks, Rev. Allison Stokes, and Rev. John Wightman.

Authors, editors, and publishers Marc Jaffe; Steven Schnur; Miriam Feinberg Vamosh; and the staff of Jewish Lights Publishing, especially Stuart M. Matlins, publisher of Jewish Lights, Alys R. Yablon, my editor, Emily Wichland, managing editor at Jewish Lights, and Jon M. Sweeney, vice president of marketing and sales.

The generous-spirited people of my congregation, Temple Anshe Amunim, especially Rebecca Aaron, Lesley Beck, Professor Steven Gerrard, Dr. Richard Greene, Rabbi Harold Salzmann, as well as Dr. Leslie Fishbein and Dolly Harte.

Above all, my parents, Sara and Meyer Mazon; my wife, Rabbi Deborah Zecher; and our three children, Josh, Adam, and Miriam. Their lives bless all my work.

—Rabbi Dennis S. Ross

INTRODUCTION

... life swings by nature
between *Thou* and *It* ...[1]

From Rush to Relation

Ten years ago, I was a rabbi at a three-thousand-family synagogue inside the Washington beltway. Between my wife and myself under one roof, our two full-time careers and three thriving children gridlocked our daily schedules with bumper-to-bumper commitments. Needing to do something to reduce the stress and strain, we decided to downsize to a small town in rural New England. There, I'd be the rabbi of a congregation a tenth the size of the previous one.

As expected, we found less traffic, fewer people, and cleaner air in the country. Much to our surprise, we also found that things haven't calmed down. After a decade in the backwoods, we are still waiting for the quiet life to begin.

At the bank, 9:05 A.M.

There are no more than four or five people ahead of me at the bank teller, but I *have* to fidget—folding, unfolding, and refolding my arms. Cranky news addict that I am, even the wall-mounted visual pacifier of a news ticker fails to further distract my already distracted attention. My body is at the bank, but my mind—patience at zero balance and little interest—is at the temple, on pastoral visits, meetings, an evening dinner program, and more in the day ahead.

"Next, please."

Finally! I recognize the teller, but from where? Slapping down checks, deposit slip, and a driver's license as identification for cash back, I force out a cheerful and convincing "Good morning!" and turn my eyes to the news ticker to avoid the time and effort of conversation.

"Put back the license!" she offers with half a chuckle. "I know just who you are. Your son was wonderful in the high school play!"

"Why ... thank you!"

How embarrassing, I think. When I tried to ignore her, the bank teller punctured my self-preoccupation with a compliment! The fidgeting suddenly disappears. Instinctively, I put aside the obsession with my own calendar and ask about *her* kids. We talk a little more, and soon the pressures of the day's appointments might as well be in someone else's date book. Then we say goodbye.

Leaving the bank, I reflect: A half minute of chit-chat with a semi-stranger offers a small example of the spirituality between people that Martin Buber called the *I-Thou* relationship.

The *I-Thou* encounter appears in a variety of circumstances. You stop by the hospital to visit a friend after surgery. Entering the room, you take notice of how sluggish and tired your friend appears. Nevertheless, you jump into a conversation that flows all by itself. As you take your leave, the positive change in your friend's emotions is obvious. The renewed animation in speech and the uplift in spirit are signs that *I-Thou* passed between the two of you.

Or you are traveling alone on an airplane, with an hour more until the flight and a half-finished novel that turned out to be a dud are done. There seems to be nothing to do—until you strike up an animated conversation with the stranger in the next seat. You get to talking about family, work, and the like. You lose track of where you are, how much longer the flight will last, where you came from, and where you are going. What was boring has become interesting, and before you realize it, your airplane has landed. This all-consuming conversation is also an *I-Thou* encounter.

Just as a suspension bridge spans an expanse between two shores, the *I-Thou* relationship is a bridge of words spanning the space between people. And, most important, at the same time we build that interpersonal bridge, we build a bridge to God in *Eternal Thou*. As Buber describes it, "With every *Thou* we are stirred with a breath of the *Thou*, that is, eternal life."² When we speak to people we also speak to God.

To Lower Hands and Join Them

Stories teach faith. Two to three hundred years ago, short stories—parables describing the wisdom and acts of the Hasidic masters—circulated around Europe. In the first four decades of the twentieth century, Martin Buber collected and edited these Hasidic stories for his book *Tales of the Hasidim*, which addresses the spiritual challenges of our time.

Throughout the book you hold in your hands, I have interlaced Buber's wonderfully retold Hasidic tales with my own stories, inviting you to weave yours in with ours. All of life's little exchanges, as well as the larger ones, can bring a breath of fresh air to a smothered, gasping spirit and leave a lasting and significant spiritual influence. This guide should help you see the stories of your life and your part in a much bigger whole.

But not everyone achieves this peace of mind and sense of place in the universe. For many of us, with too many things to do and too many places to be, our inborn spiritual potential gets lost in the rush and shuffle. Rabbi Israel ben Eliezer, also known as the Baal Shem Tov ("The Master of the Good Name") and as the founder of Hasidism, a mystical movement that originated in Eastern Europe three hundred years ago, said: "The world is filled with enormous lights and mysteries, and a person shuts them out with one small hand!"[3] In other words, just as the smaller moon blocks the larger sun in a solar eclipse, petty pressures and serious challenges of the small hand of daily living conceal the light of *I-Thou* in a spiritual eclipse. Just as the moon can cloak the sun, a handful of worldly concerns—both trivial and important—can block the eye, fill the mind, and shroud the soul. With this book, I hope to lower the eclipsing hand to reveal "enormous lights and mysteries," addressing our internal conflict at the bank counter as well as in more challenging moments of life.

A solar eclipse does not last forever. After a few minutes, the moon passes and daylight returns. But a spiritual eclipse can persist for hours, years, even a lifetime. As for the anxieties and worries that encrust the spirit, the Baal Shem Tov and the other Hasidic masters attempted to pull back the hand and end the eclipse by revealing the "enormous lights and mysteries," similar to Martin Buber's important teaching of *I-Thou*.

To a spirit lost in the dark, Rabbi Hayyim of Zanz related:

> A person lost the way in a great forest. After a while another lost the way and chanced upon the first and, without knowing what had happened, asked the way out of the woods. "I don't know," said the first. "But I can point out the ways that lead further into the thicket, and after that let us try to find the way together."[4]

When we wander the forests among home, the bank, and the office, Rabbi Hayyim would have us remove hands mislaid—not to strike one another, not to push one another away, or to grab at the goods, but to join those hands in a holy relationship.

Beyond Abandonment into Relationship: A Little Bit about Martin Buber

The idea for this book arose twenty-five years ago on a chilly, rainy winter afternoon in Jerusalem not far from the home of the late Martin Buber. As a graduate rabbinic student on an hour's break from study, I left my unheated apartment for fresh bread and the afternoon Hebrew newspaper. In no hurry to return to those chilly stone walls and bare tile floors, I wandered into a used bookstore and came upon a worn copy of Buber's *Tales of the Hasidim: Later Masters*.

"A bargain!" I thought, reaching for the Israeli equivalent of fifty cents. Little did I understand how much more than my money's worth I got that day, for this yellowing paperback would open a door to the spirit for me. Through this used book, as well as Buber's classic *I and Thou* and other works by and about him, I came to better understand the concepts and living realities of *I-Thou, I-It,* and *Eternal Thou*—ideas at the heart of this book.

Martin Buber was born in Vienna, Austria, in 1878, the only child in a middle-class household. Later in life, Buber thought back to his very early years, to memories as serene as the gently flowing Danube River canal, whose blue waters he studied from his apartment window. In that picture-book neighborhood of homes, fields, and trees nestled along the riverbank, any hint of sadness hung as far away as the distant foothills of the Alps.

People are often surprised to learn of the horrible emotional trauma Buber suffered in early childhood. When Martin was three, his mother suddenly and inexplicably disappeared, leaving Martin with a heartache that endured for the remaining eight decades of his life. Carl Buber, Martin's father, sent the little boy to live with his grandparents on their estate in rural Galicia. Martin received no explanation about his situation. In the coming years, he retained contact with his father but had none with his mother, seeing her again only once more in his adult life.

The loving attention of his grandparents helped Buber overcome this early tragedy. In addition to managing the daily details of the family's farm and mines, his grandmother, Adele Buber, oversaw her young grandson's secular education and engaged private tutors, who focused on languages and liberal arts. His grandfather, Solomon Buber, freed from daily involvement in the family business thanks to his wife, turned to Jewish scholarship and community involvement. As a noted Hebraist, he studied and edited midrash, Jewish folklore. His volumes remain in wide use today. Solomon Buber occasionally brought Martin to prayer services at the Hasidic synagogue in nearby Sadgora, attended by descendants of the founders of Hasidism. His grandparents' loving introduction to secular academics, Hebrew language, and Jewish community set the stage for Martin's spiritual development.

Buber returned to live with his father and went on to study at several European universities. During his college days, Buber joined the early Zionist movement, supporting the reestablishment of a Jewish homeland. Shortly there-after, as an adult, he returned to Hasidism in a spiritual exploration that shaped much of his thought and writing. In 1938, at the age of sixty, Buber fled Nazi Europe for Israel, accepting a professorship in social philosophy at Hebrew University in Jerusalem. After retiring in 1951, he traveled, lectured, and wrote extensively until his death in 1965.

In 1923, Martin Buber released his most important book, *I and Thou*—the culmination of his life experience, academic training, and religious explorations. In *I and Thou*, Buber distinguished between the impersonal and businesslike relationships he called the *I-It* experience and the fuller per-sonal relationships of life he called the *I-Thou* encounter. *I and Thou*, the backbone of the book you are holding, was shaped by Buber's encounter with Hasidism.

A Little Bit about Hasidism

The Baal Shem Tov founded Hasidim in the eighteenth century. He and his disciples distanced themselves from the urban, elitist Jewish mainstream thought and practice of those days. Instead of feeding dry, academic ideas to the intellect, Hasidism exalted the soul with energetic worship, joyous dancing, and fervent singing.

Hasidism brought an impassioned, spiritual Judaism to poor, hardworking Jews. Aided by the popularity of thousands of short, playful anecdotes about the charismatic Hasidic rabbis, Hasidism spread quickly across the small towns of central and western Europe. Martin Buber collected and edited these stories for his book *Tales of the Hasidim*.

In Buber's typical Hasidic tale, a disciple questions the rabbi-master about a verse of Bible or some quirk of daily life. In asking the question, the disciple unknowingly reveals something about himself to the perceptive master; choice of topic, phrasing, and language point to the disciple's internal struggle. Having faced the same issues, the master listens on two levels: an apparent, practical level and a veiled, inner level. Reacting from his living soul more than from a set of rules or tradition, the master responds in a down-to-earth and playful manner that sensitively addresses the disciple's needs, both superficial and deep.

Hasidism emphasized the practice of Jewish religious law, which never had much appeal for Buber. Instead, Buber found Hasidism spiritually appealing. He admired the deep and full relationship between the Hasidic master and each disciple. While the master did not live life for the disciples, he assumed a personal measure of responsibility for the well-being of each one. Buber was also taken by the intimate spiritual bonds within the closely knit Hasidic community—peer relationships that the master modeled and encouraged. Finally, for Buber and for us, Hasidism teaches that it is possible to infuse every moment of life with holiness, from the routine act to the once-in-a-lifetime situation. Salvation is here and now, in lacing a boot and in the final moments of life.

The fundamental elements of that classic of Jewish theology, *I and Thou*—holiness in relationships, the potential for goodness in the individual, the importance of here and now—first came to life for Buber in that tiny Hasidic synagogue in the town of Sadgora, a community built on deeply caring relationships.

The involved presence of other people—grandparents, tutors, the spiritual community of Sadgora—addressed and eased Buber's longing, a heartache that must have seemed boundless and eternal. Wholesome and strong relationships taught Buber to trust again. And in that closeness to others, Buber came closer to God, to the possibility of enduring spirituality between people.

The loving advice of master to disciple—evidence of spiritual mentoring—as expressed and recorded in Buber's Hasidic tales, can lead to the realization of the divinity in our relationships. It is my hope that this book also speaks to those aspiring to be masters and those who, unbeknownst to themselves, are masters already.

PART ONE

Our Daily Encounters

—∞∞∞—

ALWAYS UNEXPECTED

... ready on every occasion to become *Thou* ...[1]

At the office, 10:40 A.M.

"Phone for you."

I put aside the morning mail. A rabbi learns to expect interruptions.

"I was admitted to the hospital as an emergency," I hear from a friend. "And I just learned that I'm facing a life-threatening illness."

Stunned, I barely attend to the stammered description of treatment options and chances of success.

"I'll be over in a little bit."

Within the hour, struggling with shock and disbelief, I leave the office. My heart races, and my stomach is braced.

The hospital is a planet within a planet, with its own customs and rules. Entering the building, I hold the door for a man on crutches with a bandaged foot. Even in my rush, I console myself that I haven't lost all my patience and dignity. Knowing the room number, I head straight for the elevator. I hit the UP button and reread the sign: "Our staff respects privacy by not discussing our patients in public areas." Two doctors approach and drop their conversation to a whisper. Within ten seconds, we three squeeze into an elevator along with an empty gurney and its accompanying orderly. The doctors stop talking altogether, and the four of us, as if sedated, stare in silence at the closing door.

Off the elevator, I pass the waiting area for families of patients in surgery. Each longing eye meets mine as if I might bring word of a loved one's condition. In the hall, a hunched-over young man shuffles by me; his wife holds one arm, and an IV pole drags next to the other. I hear a shout from a patient's room: "You rang for help. Do you need to urinate?" At the nurses' station, the staff rough-handles and scribbles on those aluminum-clad charts, reminding me of the shouts and gestures of stock dealers on the trading floor. A nurse, oblivious to the clamorous exchange, makes a careful pill count at a medicine cart. All of this occurs under very bright fluorescent lights, brighter than the sun on a clear day. I stop within a few feet of the room, check the number, breathe in and out, and enter. By now, it's as if the conversation with the bank teller had happened last month to someone else.

My friend looks the same, though out of place in a hospital gown and bed. I say, "Other people wind up here, not you," and our conversation continues, all by itself, into gentle, sad, thoughtful, down-to-earth reflections about how family and friends are taking the news, and worries about the office and what the future will bring—all laced with realism, resignation, and regret. We ramble from topic to topic, disagree over a couple of things, even challenge each other—and it's all okay. The eyes say everything—from a wink to a raised brow, a blink to tears of concern. Close as we are, we have never spoken like this before.

Focused on the conversation, we pay no attention to surrounding distractions. We don't comment on the mixed aroma of rubbing alcohol and arriving lunch, a message that tells the patient to work up an appetite while cringing for an injection. We ignore the whooshing and beeping of hospital equipment, the roommate's loud phone argument, and the housekeeper fussing over the trash basket. We lose track of our location, the time, and the reason we are sitting together in the first place. Past and future collapse into here and now. With the riveting back-and-forth, I hardly notice that the knot in my stomach has loosened.

"It's the best a person could do," I offer, preparing to take leave. "It's wise to put off any decision until we get more information. We don't want this, but we have to deal with it, and that's what we will do, together. I'll be back tomorrow. Call if you need anything."

From *I-It* Experience to *I-Thou* Encounter

**I-*Thou* arouses memories,
but memories are not *I-Thou*.**

Passing the nurse's station, I ignore the continuing commotion. My world feels very different from the way it did when I reached the hospital. Anxiety about what will happen is blended with resignation over what might well be. Admiration for a friend's strength infiltrates my worry. A determination to remain present through it all, to hang in there, no matter what, squeezes down my fear. A friend has taken comfort in my willingness to be there.

As I walk down the hall, I think back to my father's death at the age of thirty-five, to the anxious uncertainty I experienced. The thoughts that flashed through my ten-year-old mind have persistently replayed themselves over the decades. I often enter these aftershocks of the untimely and unjust shattering of childhood peace, reexperiencing snippets of the confusion, shame, guilt, and anger of those troubling days. Whenever I go to the hospital or get a call for a funeral, it's as if someone is making me watch an old, worn, emotionally intense videotape.

Walking along, I peek into a neighboring room. A patient, entranced by a TV soap opera, absentmindedly munches on the contents of a king-sized bag of potato chips, chewing slowly, fully, and mechanically, the way I've nibbled away at a tub of popcorn at the movies. Absorbed in the film, it's not until the bottom of the tub that I feel any sadness at all, when a lull in the action blends with regret for what was barely tasted and only now appreciated in its absence.

That faint sense of loss echoes my more powerful forty-year-old memory of losing my father. While he was alive, in my relationship with him I was like a wakeful sleepwalker. And when he was gone, rather than feel the gratitude for what was, I mourned his absence and felt a sorrowful hankering for life only half-lived and half-enjoyed, taken for granted and longed for only because it was gone.

Some Differences

between

I-It and *I-Thou*

**I-It is in facts and figures,
where *I-Thou* is in relation.**

When it comes to offering a medical diagnosis or performing surgery, everything lies in the hands of the doctors and the hospital staff. A visit from a rabbi, a relative, or a good friend offers no promise that sickness will go away and that a loved one will return to health—or even survive. But on another level, being *present*, wholeheartedly sharing an open and honest conversation, can have a tremendous influence on a person in crisis. It is this presence that Martin Buber called *I-Thou*.

I meets *Thou* in the night's trauma as in the morning's joy. At the hospital bedside, when words rise from one soul and enter another, and at the bank, when a chance comment elevates a work-worn spirit, in peak moments and in the daily routine abides a spirituality—the same kind of *presence* between people called *I-Thou*.

It is best to understand the *I-Thou* encounter as it compares with the *I-It* experience. As we see *I-Thou* and *I-It* in contrast, we come to better realize the significance of each.

Imagine two people at the beach. One person studies the water, estimates the wave height, calculates the times of high tide and low, measures the humidity and the air temperature, and checks out the size of the crowd on such a hot day. In this *I-It experience*, writes Buber, "with the magnifying glass of peering observation [a person] bends over particulars and objectifies them, or with the field-glass of remote inspection he objectifies them and arranges them as scenery."[2] While the first person stands there and *experiences I-It*, the second person jumps into the water for a swim. And this is the way we *encounter* in *I-Thou*. Where *I-It* experiences as an onlooker, *I-Thou* encounters as a participant. And there is even more difference between the two approaches to relationships.

Whereas *I-Thou* encounters the *whole*, *I-It* experiences a *portion*. *I-It* classifies people like water (cold or salty, turbulent or placid) or like sand (coarse or gritty). A human being is reduced to a suit size, an account number, just another faceless clerk in a cage, an unusual hair color, a given level of education, a career path, a gender, or a sexual orientation. Mechanical, all business, cold and impersonal—*I-It* categorizes and analyzes people, putting human beings into mental cubbyholes.

In *I-It*, a meteorologist looks at the clouds and forecasts the next day's weather. A financial advisor studies past stock market performance and estimates how well a client's investment portfolio is doing. A pollster surveys and tallies

public opinion to predict the results of an upcoming elec-
tion. In dealing with people, the *I-It* experience treats a
person like a thing to "compare it with objects, establish it
in its order among classes of objects, describe and analyze
it objectively."[3] In *I-It*, a doctor looks into the eye, sees a
retina, and diagnoses a medical condition; that's easy to
comprehend. In *I-Thou*, a friend gazes into the same eye
but responds to the soul, and this point is not easy to grasp
or explain.

I-It is just about any kind of intellectual exercise. The *I-
It* experience is concerned with facts. In *I-It*, we learn
about love from a book. The *I-Thou* encounter is about
real life. We step into *I-Thou* when we enter loving relationships.

In the academic inquiry of *I-It*, we get information
about God from listening to a lecture. In the free and honest *I-Thou* encounter, we get closer to God by living, by
striking up a conversation as we might jump in for a swim,
hitting the water and letting it happen.

BUBER'S THEOLOGY OF RELATIONSHIPS

I-Thou: **Personal yet between people,
an inborn capability refined by
living, universal and individual,
ephemeral, and also eternal.**

Albert Einstein, Buber's friend, helped us understand the world through the *I-It* constructs of scientific theory and mathematical formulas. Although not at all dis-missive of Einstein's approach, Buber's theology of relationships turns to the world via encounter. Ultimately, Buber was not concerned with chemical composition or atomic structure. Buber did not busy himself with the economic law of supply and demand or the "scientific ordering of nature."[4] And unlike students of psychology, Buber was not interested in dissecting the human soul to uncover hidden memories, the source of a person's anger, or recollections of earliest life experiences. Martin Buber taught us how to live, fully and in the present, in *I-Thou*.

By now, at least one thing should be clear about *I-Thou*. Although easily entered, *I-Thou* is a challenge to comprehend and explain. With *I-Thou*, you "can give no account at all of how the binding in relation is brought about ... you have no formula or picture for it."[5]

I-Thou is hard to describe, in part because of the way Buber communicates his ideas. Buber usually wrote in his native German—a difficult language for English speakers to penetrate, even with good translation. In addition, he even joked about going out of his way to make simple ideas appear complex.

Buber is hard to follow for another reason: *I-Thou* ends the moment we begin to describe it. As one's reflection disappears when one steps away from a mirror, *I-Thou* wanders off as soon it is discussed. *I-Thou*, written about in a book, becomes *I-It*. Although no description does *I-Thou* justice, we can speak from a Jewish perspective to all faiths about the inborn and delicate spirituality *between* people. We can begin with a few important points about *I-Thou*:

- The *I-Thou* encounter is interpersonal. In the quest for spiritual fulfillment, many seekers look into the soul. *I-Thou* undertakes this spiritual quest from a different perspective, turning the soul *outward* to the spirituality not in the speaker or listener but *between* them.

- People do not need much knowledge or experience to encounter one another in *I-Thou*; we are born with the ability. *I-Thou* demands no special training, spiritual discipleship, or seminary education. Although *I-Thou* comes naturally, it can benefit from a little assistance.

- The *I-Thou* encounter is universal. *I-Thou* is for people of all faiths, countries, and continents. Establishing a vision for communication and cooperation—across a dinner table or across an international border—*I-Thou* promises a way to banish human estrangement and bring about world peace.

* Finally, the *I-Thou* encounter is easily overlooked. Because *I-Thou* opens quietly, rises softly, and closes modestly, it often goes unrecognized. People enter and leave *I-Thou* without even realizing it.

Thus, we find *I-Thou* along all the hills and valleys of life and along all points in between, from extreme to routine. Interhuman, innate, and universal, *I-Thou* is the portal to God. Yes, *I-Thou* leads us to divinity, but *I-It* sets the stage for the journey.

I-It is the birthplace of *I-Thou*. *I-It* is the food, shelter, and clothing we need to go about life. It is the good health, the comfortable chair, and the satisfying meal that prepare us for entering confidently in our relationships. The *I-It* experience is the first home of the *I-Thou* encounter.

I-It: The Cradle

of *I-Thou*

**The *It* is the eternal chrysalis,
the *Thou* the eternal butterfly.**[6]

At the hospital, 11:50 A.M.
Under the heaviness of the previous hospital visit, I stop at
a pay phone to check messages at the office.

"Your roofer called. He's starting work on Monday."

"What a relief!"

In a moment, I shift from the *I-Thou* of a hospital bedside to the *I-It* of home repair. In my rapid transition, was I
being disrespectful, insensitive to a friend's suffering? Was I
repressing a larger, psychological issue? Is there something
wrong when mundane responsibilities of roofing or banking
juxtapose with questions of life and death?

As I mentioned earlier, Buber's family said very little to him
about his mother's disappearance when he was a child. Several
years after the abandonment, Martin was once left with a
caretaker. He recalled standing alongside a railing when his
caretaker simply and bluntly noted that his mother would
never return. A stunned, silent Buber knew his sitter was
right. He finally had to accept the truth about his mother.

A sad destiny is embedded in *I-Thou*: "The exalted melancholy of our fate, that every *Thou* in our world must become an *It*."[7] The cold reality of the sitter's comment clutched Martin's soul, and as he grew into adulthood the grip on his spirit tightened. He realized the stark truth in his sitter's words: No *I-Thou* relationship endures forever; "the bright *Thou* appeared and was gone."[8] As short-lived as it is deeply cherished, as desirable as it is temporary, *I-Thou* is destined to wither away as surely as it comes to life.

In the wake of the abandonment by his mother, Buber further learned that the end of every relationship is built into the beginning. The *I-Thou* relationship inevitably yields to the *I-It* experience. At the moment of taking leave from that friend, whether at the hospital bedside or at the bank counter, parting ways for a day or forever, *I-Thou* unravels. Such is the tragedy of the human condition.

A person might be tempted to fight the lapse of *I-Thou* into *I-It*, but Buber cautions us: *I-It* is the "chrysalis," the cocoon, the birthplace of *I-Thou*. If you want the *I-Thou* of the butterfly, you have to accept the *I-It* of the cocoon. The Rabbi of Kobryn once gazed skyward and lamented: "Angel, little angel! ... Just you come down to earth and worry about eating and drinking, about raising children and earning money, and we shall see if you keep being an angel."[9] *I-It* is unavoidable—and it is also essential. We are mortals, not angels. We need to eat and drink, to have places to live and clothing to wear—we need a cocoon. We need a cradle for the baby. Welcome to the better side of *I-It*, the side we cannot live without.

I-It and *I-Thou* in Professional and Helping Relationships

I-Thou needs *I-It,* the imbalance and the restrictions.

We knew we'd need a new roof when we bought the house. A recent leak in an upstairs closet made the need more urgent. After the Yellow Pages, estimates and references, discussions of chimney flashing and shingle color, our *I-It* preoccupations culminated in a signed contract.

The following Monday, when the roofer showed up at my doorstep, we didn't swap life stories or pictures of the children in the realm of *I-Thou.* I signed a deposit check, and he got to work to pay for the roof over *his* own head. In this case, *I-It,* necessary for life, is not negative, even when it curtails the possibility of entering an *I-Thou* relationship.

We cannot live life without *I-It,* without the technical language of soffits and eaves, joists and flashing. *I-It* charges by the hour or works on commission, follows instructions, and sticks to the schedule. Timed and measured, confined to a space, planned and analyzed, *I-It* catches trains, answers phones, and logs on to the Internet. Try paying the mortgage without the money *I-It* brings. When a roofer estimates costs or discovers rot in the rafters, when a doctor determines the cause of a backache, "Aha!" marks the productive *I-It* of examination and discovery.

I wanted to be *It* when I showed up in the emergency room with a stomach cramp and a fever. Yes, I also wanted that little bit of *I-Thou* of reassurance when the nurse said, "We are going to take good care of you, right away." But ultimately, I wanted to be nothing more than an MRI scan to the radiologist, whom I trusted to have the training, skill, experience, and undistracted time to read the test results just right. We do not run away from *I-It*, nor do we stamp it out and repress it. We try to use it, get the better of it, channel its energies into serving holy purposes.

I-It is often marked by a knowledge imbalance or a power differential. I don't know much about roofing. The roofer has the skill and experience that I lack. A doctor has the training, experience, and skill to diagnose a disease. The relationship between the professional, who knows the business, and the client, who is ignorant and wants the professional's help, is not equal. The patient does not go to a doctor to hear about the doctor's illness; the patient wants a one-way relationship. The sick person wants professional advice and turns to a doctor for that informed opinion. This inequality is part of the healthier side of *I-It*—the side we need.

I-It is necessary, and the imbalance of the *I-It* relationship is crucial. Sometimes people assume that the boss and the workers must be good chums, that professional and client must be on equal *I-Thou* terms to succeed, that student and teacher must learn together, therapist and client must make simultaneous discoveries. These are all nice ideas, but impractical. When we are dealing with *I-Thou*, professional parity is not only unnecessary but potentially harmful.

When a person seeks a counselor—a rabbi, a minister, or a psychotherapist—the counselor sees the problem and the answer, while the seeker barely understands the problem, let alone knows what to do with it. When the doctor diagnoses a patient's illness, it may well be an illness the patient does not recognize, let alone know how to treat. And when the doctor gives the patient medication and information, that moment of teaching and healing is also *I-It. I-It* works *because I-It* is unequal.

An *I-Thou* encounter can grow out of an unequal *I-It*. For instance, psychotherapy begins as *I-It*. It is easy to immediately recognize the *I-It* of psychotherapy when the first session opens: one person wants the help of the other and is willing to pay a fee to be heard and to receive advice. This financial and professional imbalance speaks *I-It* experience; no parity here. Through a therapist's careful listening and measured response, the client heals, entering *I-Thou* with the therapist. But we need more. A "psychotherapist ... may be successful in some repair work ... [but] the regeneration of an atrophied personal center ... can only be attained in the person-to-person attitude of a partner.[10] The client, with soul strengthened from meeting the *Thou* of the therapist as an *I*, leaves the therapist's office and faces the world of people better prepared to enter into fuller relationships and fuller spiritual health.

The human services professional has to develop and maintain careful self-awareness. For instance, when I teach, I learn something from my students, but *my* education is not the reason

I stand at the front of the classroom. I gain insight from people who seek my advice, but I counsel them primarily for their sake and not for the sake of my spiritual growth. A relationship between clergy and congregant may become *I-Thou*.

Whereas *I-Thou* is open and free, *I-It* follows the rules. We need the structure, direction, and chain of command, from foreman to carpenters to cleanup crew. *I-It* is in the instructions a boss imposes on a worker. It is the force that allows people to form productive and successful teams. As the job descriptions of *I-It* circumscribe the behavior of workers, similar work rules also regulate the behavior of management. *I-It* protects the employees and customers through professional standards and experienced supervision, fair wages, and timely payment. The *I-It* of the employee manual even provides insurance in case someone is injured on the job.

Counselors, teachers, and clergy serve under professional codes of ethics to prevent abuses and protect the less-empowered innocent. Rules need to direct the power of *I-It*, setting up restraints to hold the passions in check and prevent the less powerful from being harmed. The regulations and sanctions imposed by outside organizations ensure that a skewed relationship stays honest and does not exploit the less empowered. The rule book often cuts off the possibility of a fuller relationship.

I-It: Limited and Seductive

**Where *I-Thou* accepts and respects
the whole person, *I-It* sees people as
implements—or impediments—to a goal
and risks of exploitation.**

I-It is good, but not good enough. In his college days, Martin Buber joined the Zionist movement and went on to become the editor of the group's newspaper. The Zionist leadership emphasized the politics of securing a safe refuge for oppressed Jews. Eventually, Buber saw the shortcomings of such a narrow political approach. He believed that there was more to being human than an address and a native tongue. He believed that as much as a Jewish state needed land, it also needed Jewish spirit imbued with Jewish ideals such as justice, democracy, and mercy, and Jewish culture—literature, art, music, and the Hebrew language. Always a Zionist, Buber lived his final years in Jerusalem, all the while teaching that a State of Israel—like any nation—needs to provide something more for the spirit than placing people into little compartments of religion or language. His experience with political

Zionism pointed to the limits of a purely *I-It* approach to
life.

Buber well understood the seductive dangers of *I-It.*
When *I-It* employs a person as a tool to achieve a higher
goal, personal feelings go into lockdown. No words leave the
heart, and no thoughts touch the soul. Yes, there is good in
I-It, and we must live with the little bit of bad in *I-It.* All
the while we must recognize that *I-It* has the potential to
become exploitative and unethical—for instance, when a
person "sees the beings around ... as machines, capable of
various achievements, which must be ... utilised for the
Cause."[11]

Sometimes, and sadly, people act on the temptation to
use power to exploit others and satisfy their own needs. It
is then that the *I-It* of propaganda offers the official word,
dishes up spin, churns out disinformation to induce everyone to think the "right way." *I-It* lobbies for legislation.
The *I-It* of gossip or of a sales pitch, disguised by false sin-
cerity, is a one-sided deal. When the doctor's patient
becomes just another knee, when the roofer just slaps
down the shingles to get home sooner, or when I *must*
make a good impression on my dinner companion, life
darkens and the spirit hardens. *I-It* bubbles up to swamp
and smother delicate and fragile *I-Thou,* claiming an easy
and tragic victory.

I-It Darkens and Hardens

The transition between
I-Thou and *I-It*
can be gentle or jarring.

At the hospital, 11:55 A.M.
As I hang up the hospital lobby telephone I overhear a few words spoken into the next telephone—a loud conversation I tried to shut out in order to pay attention to my own.

"Honey!" I hear with more sting than sweetness. "If you can't pick up the car from the auto body shop, then what good are you to me?"

I think back to the very first lesson I learned as a day camp counselor-in-training: criticize the behavior, not the person. When a child becomes a "bad kid" instead of a kid who sometimes does bad things, when my spouse becomes "my driver" and nothing else, the spirit darkens, and *I-Thou* enters eclipse.

I-It is good and useful, necessary and acceptable. Because it is open to the possibility of exploitation and abuse, *I-It* also requires a delicate balance. When emotions are not understood, or when they get out of hand, a person becomes a tool to achieving my agenda, and the light of *I-Thou* disappears.

PART TWO

I-It: A Spirit in Eclipse— Seven Stories

ECLIPSED BY THE RACE

**If a [person] lets it have the mastery,
the continually growing world of *It*
overruns him and robs him of
the reality of his own *I*, till the incubus ...
and the ghost within ...
whisper to one another
the confession of their non-salvation.**[1]

Our home is in the country, beside a brook, surrounded by grass and trees. Summer foliage hides our yard from the neighbors. Come winter, with fallen leaves, we gaze between the bare branches into the neighbor's large field and watch horses romp and race.

On occasion, I must go to the city. Rising before the sun, I leave the quiet, wooded neighborhood for a two-hour drive to catch a crowded commuter train and, if my luck holds, get a seat.

Approaching the city, the packed train descends from elevated tracks into a dark tunnel beneath the street, beneath traffic, pedestrians, high-rise apartments, and offices. Nearing the last stop, the train slows down, signaling the regular riders to tuck newspapers under arms, place manila folders in attaché cases, secure laptop computers, rise to remove coats and hats from overhead racks, and stroll to exit doors to wait. The standing commuters' hangdog heads gently rock to the car's sway. Eyes droop as if the conductor were instructing the group to meditate. I accept the unspoken invitation to rise and join in.

Brakes squeal, the train halts, and doors rattle open. We race from the platform, into the waiting rooms, and up to the street as if a homing beam were entrancing each consciousness, commandeering each body through the crowd to an assigned work cubicle. "[I]n times of sickness it comes about that the world of *It,* no longer penetrated and fructified by the inflowing world of *Thou* as by living streams ... hardens into the world of *It.*"[2] The office is open, but the spirit, worn raw, is closed, eclipsed into *I-It* by the daily race.

ECLIPSED BY THE EQUIPMENT

**What a person earns and owns
eclipses what that person can be.**

Take another train with me.

Years ago, I attended Hebrew Union College–Jewish Institute of Religion in New York City. Introducing the thoughts of Martin Buber, Rabbi Eugene Borowitz asked us to picture a clerk sitting in a dark, tiny cage of an underground subway token booth, selling those little round coins for the turnstile. Passenger after passenger slides change under the window bars and grunts at the clerk. The clerk in the shadow box passes back a token, along with another grunt—no extra charge. But along comes a token purchaser who offers words instead of grunts, who says to the bored and tired clerk, "I hope you get off work early today to enjoy some of that fine weather up there."

Suddenly, there is a new and fresh mood in the booth. Clerk and purchaser exchange a few more words, warm words. The conversation is over in a flash. Brief as it was, the sharing of words—real words—nevertheless fit the definition of what Martin Buber called the *I-Thou* relationship.

Any simple conversation, even between strangers, can be marked by uplift, hope, and caring.

Take one more train, this one with the Hasidic masters.

As the nineteenth century ended, an industrial revolution transformed daily life in Europe's larger cities, while the backwoods Jewish villages, known as shtetls, sustained themselves as always: by the hand-cultivated and the handmade. Engines of mass production, electrification, and steam power brought tremendous change to material life in the urban areas, while the isolated shtetl underwent a spiritual renewal, thanks to the groundswell of Hasidism.

Rabbi Abraham Yaakov, of the shtetl Sadgora, reflected on the nagging spiritual problems imposed by the newly born industrial age and on the mismatch in the marriage of human being and modern machine. Rabbi Abraham Yaakov remarked that every one of God's creations has something to teach, adding that the things people make also offer a lesson:

> "What can we learn from a train?" one Hasid asked dubiously.
> "That because of one second one can miss everything."
> "And from the telegraph?"
> "That every word is counted and billed."
> "And the telephone?"
> "That what we say here is heard there."[3]

No train stopped in Sadgora, no telephones rang across the hinterlands of Romania, but Rabbi Abraham Yaakov recognized the spiritual costs imposed by those modern brainchildren: Timing becomes everything, payment goes

by the word, and speech reverberates beyond the horizon—
all at the expense of the human spirit.

Riding rails or traveling the roads, then and today, the
struggle is the same. Once, Rabbi Levi Yitzhak of Berditchev
observed a man hurrying along the street, looking neither
right nor left:

> "Why are you rushing so?" he asked him.
>
> "I am after my livelihood," the man replied.
>
> "And how do you know," continued the rabbi, "that
> your livelihood is running on before you, so that you
> have to rush after it? Perhaps it is behind you, and
> all you need do to encounter it is to stand still."[4]

Scratching out that livelihood—along the dirt roads of
Berditchev or onto pads of yellow paper from a perch in
the city's concrete canyons—leaves little time or energy for
life. With blinders on the soul and eyes on the tracks, a
person races across town without looking right or left.
With "the decrease of the [person's] power to enter into
relation,"[5] the spirit enters eclipse.

Today's electronic inventions have further complicated
the problems that Rabbi Abraham Yaakov and Rabbi Levi
Yitzhak addressed—conflicts that arose when we harnessed
fire and discovered the wheel. Human history is marked by
"a progressive augmentation of the world of It."[6] Machines
that were designed to care for us force us to care for them.
Timesaving gadgets ring and beep, and we jump to do their
bidding. Now that bodies, possessions, and ideas travel
faster than ever, our accessories turn us into their
appendages, and the old struggle between person and
creation grows ever more intense. Unable to cope with the

consequences of our creations, we might recall the Hasidic story of the lost traveler wandering the woods, alone in the dark, despairing of ever joining hands or ever finding the way out of the thicket. The darkness of *I-It* can isolate and befuddle the soul.

Eclipsed by the Pace

**Where and how a soul travels eclipses
what that soul might have become.**

Today we yearn for a slower pace, for a daily life less encumbered and less interrupted. Some two centuries ago, a road-worn Rabbi Menahem Mendel of Rymanov reminisced about the relative quiet and calm of earlier times:

> As long as there were no roads, you had to interrupt a journey at nightfall. Then, you had all the leisure in the world to recite psalms at the inn, to open a book and to have a good talk with one another. But nowadays you can ride on these roads day and night and there is no peace anymore.[7]

On the road that never closes, a travel-weary Rabbi Menahem Mendel paid a toll in "psalms ... a book ... a good talk." A victim of the struggle between spirit and technology, he lamented the lost pleasures of cultivating the soul, nourishing the mind, and chatting with a friend.

It was a spiritual challenge to balance machine and mortal when the horse-drawn wagon plied the dirt roads around Berditchev, Sadgora, and Rymanov. It is an ever more complicated challenge on the interstate today, when darkness overtakes the always-open road, and cars and trucks drone and rumble through the night under self-illumination.

Whether information technology relies on smoke signals, telephone, or fiberoptic cable, whether transportation is powered by steam, diesel, or mule, the haggard life-traveler stops for an hour, gulps a quick meal at a roadside rest stop, counts a penny or two gained or lost, and, lured by powerful engines that lull and numb the soul, returns to the concrete and asphalt. In an information age, as technological concoctions continue to overtake and overturn the old and simpler ways of getting there and being heard, an old problem gets worse: On a darkened road that never closes, amid the shouting and the clamor, the clacking and the clatter, the journey-worn traveler does not sleep, and the spirit does not waken.

There is even more to the modern crisis of spirit. Issues of the spirit, of space, of possessions, and of personal history, to name a few, can lead a person to deep despair.

Eclipsed by Itself

A self-absorbed soul eclipses itself.

What Rabbi Abraham Yaakov realized about the train, Rabbi Levi Yitzhak found on the muddy paths of Berditchev, and Rabbi Menahem Mendel discovered in the noise and the grit of the always-open road, Martin Buber observed in the quiet of his study. In early adulthood, Buber meditated regularly at home. One afternoon, a young man, seeking Buber's advice on a personal issue, interrupted Buber's reverie. Buber received his unexpected visitor, all the while remaining enraptured by the afterglow of meditation, paying little attention to the conversation. Although not ignoring his guest, Buber withheld his curiosity and responded half-heartedly. What could have been an *I-Thou* sharing fell into a self-absorbed *I-It*. And the man left with his questions unanswered.

Months later, Buber learned that his guest had died in World War I. A shocked and guilt-torn Buber reflected on a squandered spiritual opportunity. He had not honored the trust of an open soul! A fully present Buber, recognizing the despair that prompted the visit, could have offered the young man the besought life-saving meaning.

The news of the man's death, as the story goes, helped Buber realize the shortcomings of keeping to oneself and of the responsibility of wholehearted response to the next human being one encounters. Buber learned the hard way about the ethical obligation to enter into a conversation as a full partner. He saw that spiritual opportunity knocks in relationship, not in isolation; that people are not obstacles to the spirit, but paths to it.

We don't find God by turning our backs on others, by answering as defiantly as the Bible's Cain, "Am I my brother's keeper?" We meet God when we encounter in *I-Thou*, accountable, trusting, and responding in relation. Wrote Buber, "Without *It* [a person] cannot live. But [one] who lives with *It* alone is not a [person]."[8] It may be true that 80 or 90 percent of life is just showing up. But it's the last few percentage points between being there and being there fully that make a person a master.

Rabbi Yitzhak Meir of Ger pointed to the darkness of the ninth of the Ten Plagues of Egypt to illustrate this point:

> A person who does not want to look at a neighbor
> soon cleaves to one's place and is not able to move
> from it.[9]

Like a soul afflicted by a plague of darkness, we also can enter emotional lockdown, neither expressing feelings nor fully attending to the spoken word. Often seeing only ourselves, we wind up stuck in place.

A soul gets eclipsed by that battle for one's livelihood and the space for living, by the quest for site as well as size, by the armwrestle for a rung on the ladder or the corner office, instead of relating in what little space there is. On the rush-hour train and on the always-open road, the self-promoting elbow of *I-It* shoves the next person off the bench. Of those consumed by the rivalry for a better spot on the map, Rabbi Abraham Yaakov of Sadgora observed:

> "Each person has a place. Then why do people sometimes feel so crowded?"
> He replied: "Because each one wants to occupy the place of the other."[10]

If the neighbor's grass is *always* greener, I'll always want the neighbor's grass, no matter how much grass I already own. But remember: There's a spiritual cost to winning the squabble over a better seat or that room with an ocean view—the light of *I-Thou* may well become concealed.

Eclipsed by Possessions

**The "what" of ownership eclipses
the "who" of humanity.**

In the days before their financial success, Rabbi Zusya and
Rabbi Elimelech visited Ludmir and lodged with a town
resident, as poor and pious as they were. Years later, after
becoming materially successful, the rabbis returned to
Ludmir, this time riding in a fine carriage.

> The wealthiest man in that little town, who never
> wanted to have anything to do with them, came to
> meet them the moment he heard they arrived, and
> begged them to lodge in his house. But they said:
> "Nothing has changed in us to make you respect us
> more than before. What is new is just the horses
> and carriage. Take them for your guests, but let us
> stop with our old host, as usual."[11]

Rabbis Zusya and Elimelech, cherishing humanity and
decency more than possessions, stayed with the pauper
who had known them back when. Masters of the soul, they
avoided those who sized up the newcomers by the cladding
of the body, people who confused what a person owns with
who a person is.

There is no sin in enjoyment. In fact, it is a mitzvah—a religious obligation—to partake of the fruits of the earth. At the creation of the universe, God instructed Adam and Eve to make use of the world's goodness. As Judaism evolved, the Rabbis stressed the joys of the Sabbath, marking the day of rest with the best food and the best clothing while recognizing that a garment label identifies only the manufacturer, not the wearer.

How often we make more of what we own than we ought to! Yes, it's fine to enjoy what we purchase, but we must acknowledge that nothing the dollar buys will fully or permanently quench the soul's thirst. On the short-lived reassurance that comes from travel on a better set of wheels, Rabbi Moshe Leib of Sasov said, "How hard it is for a rich person to depend on God! All those possessions call out: 'Depend on us!'"[12] "Answer my page!" they call out. "Change my oil!" When self-confidence depends on a car's manufacturer or the size of an investment portfolio, the small hand of gold and silver obscures from sight the human purpose on earth and holds the spirit in eclipse.

On the distraction by material goods, Rabbi Hanoch of Alexander tells of this man:

> When he got up in the morning, it was so hard for him to find his clothes that at night he almost hesitated to go to bed for thinking of the trouble he would have on waking. One evening he finally made a great effort, took paper and pencil, and as he undressed noted down exactly where he had put everything he had on. The next morning, very well pleased with himself, he took the slip of paper in hand and read: "cap"—there it was, he set it on his

head; "pants"—there they lay, he got into them;
and so it went until he was fully dressed.

"That's all very well, but now where am I myself?"[13]

Seeing the garment, we ignore the person it clothes. Finding the goods, we lose the humanity. When life is just about living in the right neighborhood, driving the right automobile, dressing the right way, and catching the right train, when the focus becomes getting the first release of the latest gadget, when we make more of what we have than who we are, the things we own take possession of us and *I-Thou* disappears, eclipsed by the dollar and what it buys.

ECLIPSED BY THE PAST

"Here and now" becomes eclipsed by a lingering vision of what was.

Rabbi David of Lelov traveled to a distant town. A woman, mistakenly taking Rabbi David for her estranged husband, struck him. Quickly realizing her mistake, she wept:

> "Stop crying," Rabbi David said to her. "You were not striking me, but your husband." And he added in a low tone: "How often we strike someone because we take that person for another!"[14]

How often we express our anger at one person because we are angry at someone else! And how often, driven by what we were, by what our parents did to us, or by the decisions we made years ago, life becomes a self-righteous mission to right old wrongs. Smarting over festering past injustice, we as individuals or as nations punish whoever happens to be in the way. With vision skewed by grudges, recrimination, and blame, and with judgment ruled by history rather than reality, our mounting anger erupts as road rage or air rage. On a communal level, begrudging nations strike armed blows. It would be better to recognize that setbacks, painful as they may be, are the risks of living rather than wrongs to be corrected. How much better it would be to see the person who stands before us rather than the individual of long ago!

ONE VOICE
LIFTS ANOTHER

When there is no encounter of
I and *Thou*—after an eclipse of an hour,
a week, or a month—
a person can fall into despair.

As a young adult, a distraught Buber, tormented by issues of time, space, and the meaning of life, came close to suicide. Soon thereafter, he rediscovered the hope he had lost. Not every crisis of faith is so dramatic, but every one is significant. When the train never stops and the phone keeps ringing, when a soul is too tired or too distracted to engage in the few moments of conversation that would lower the hand and open the spirit, that soul remains captive to the grinding rush, stuck in place, unaware of its sorry condition.

Israel enslaved by Pharaoh in Egypt became inured to life in eclipse. As Rabbi Hanoch of Alexander said: "The real exile of Israel in Egypt was that they had learned to endure it."[15] Accustomed to suffering, Israel was convinced its misery would last forever. Nevertheless, in these moments of lost faith, one voice can lift another.

It is in the eclipse of *I-It* that we place possessions before people and see only our past and nothing of our present. During a family spat or a confrontation with a neighbor, the goodness of the next person becomes harder to identify. Tired, anxious, or misunderstood, we lose a sense of boundary and perspective. A soul becomes worn down by years of travel on the road that never ends. That person finishes the gauntlet run; sits breathless, huffing and puffing; and is unable to raise the voice. As Rabbi Pinhas of Koretz told us, *especially* in these moments of dark *I-It* experience, the master will take up the challenge to say "Thou."

> When a person is singing and cannot lift the voice and another comes and sings, another who can lift the voice, then the first will be able to lift the voice, too. That is the secret of the bond between spirit and spirit.[16]

Imagine life as a song. The despairing voice, lacking the strength to raise itself and sing, finds another voice—and both voices sing together. Even as the final moments of life approach, heartsick souls can find mutual uplift in the bond between spirit and spirit of *I* and *Thou*.

THE AFTERGLOW

Despite stifling darkness
and smothering silence,
one soul gives voice to another
through the word *Thou*.

At the hospital, 11:56 A.M.

Turning from the phone, I hear "Hey, Rabbi! How are you?"

It's the mother of last Saturday's bar mitzvah boy. It was a remarkable time for her and the family.

"I feel great! What are you doing here?" It's the question to ask whenever I run into someone at the hospital.

"Oh, I'm fine. Just a routine test."

We chat briefly and warmly about the past weekend and the bar mitzvah service. As we head our separate ways, I continue to think back on the day, the service, and the rehearsals that prepared for it.

A bar mitzvah for a boy, or a bat mitzvah for a girl, affirms a child's Jewish identity and entry into Jewish adulthood. The service, led by the young teen for the entire congregation as well as family and friends as invited guests, includes Hebrew from the Sabbath liturgy, readings from Scripture, and a speech offering a personal interpretation of the biblical lesson.

A public embrace of a religious tradition can be a daunt-ing act for a growing child. Even for an adult, it can be stressful to stand on the pulpit of a sanctuary filled with people. With the support of teachers, tutors, and a rabbi, no child ever falters. The entire experience always rein-forces the teen's ability and goodness.

Sometimes this wonderful, prayerful, and social event carries a tinge of added anxiety. At times, an overriding family issue—be it a special learning need of the child, a long-standing family disagreement, the illness of a relative, or a recent death in the family—overshadows the joy and pride of the day and calls upon my social work background more than my skills as a rabbi. The challenge becomes greater when the family or the child does not feel comfort-able discussing the issues.

As we entered the final weeks of rehearsals, this boy— her son—carried an extra measure of worry on his face. As he practiced reading from the Torah, his voice bore dry-ness. Ten days before the service, we were halfway into an hour's session, and the parents had yet to arrive to rehearse their parts. The boy fumbled with his practice sheets and his disorganized folder. When he could not find a page of his revised speech, he was on the edge of tears, as some-times happens. He seemed to be under pressure, mostly self-generated. So I offered some advice.

"There are two kinds of mistakes. The first kind is made by people who don't practice. They don't know the materi-al well because they never took the time to learn it. They don't get it right because they don't know it. You are NOT in this category. Like me, you make the second kind of mistake: when you are well rehearsed, your mind draws a blank, or you lose your place for a moment and read the wrong word. These are mistakes that everyone makes. They just can't be helped. My advice here is to do what I do: Don't look back, just keep going."

His eyes were riveted on me. Clearly, he was attending to every one of my words. So I just kept talking.

"If you are on your bike and hit a bump and you look back at the bump, what might happen?"

"If I am moving ahead, I might hit another bump, I guess. And I might fall off."

I knew I had him.

"It's the same thing here. Don't look back. Don't risk losing your balance. Keep moving ahead and, like me, you will do just fine. Any questions?"

A little smile. No words.

"Let's go ahead."

I heard announced, in a voice that had found new strength, "We continue on page 437."

My voice had lifted a spirit.

PART THREE

I-Thou:
When One Voice
Lifts Another

CHANCE ENCOUNTER

All real living is meeting.[1]

At the hospital cafeteria, 12:05 P.M.
Like a child without an appetite turning a piece of cold chicken over and over, I read and review the lunch choices. Amid the discordant arrhythmia of tableware rattling on lunch trays and serving utensils striking the aluminum steamer table, out of this unsyncopated cacophony of kitchen rap, I hear, "Rabbi, sitting with anyone?"

It's a doctor. We know each other from a hospital committee we serve on.

"That would be great. I'd enjoy it."

I have no idea what we will talk about. I can tell you where our relationship has been but not where it will go. All a person can do is anticipate.

We barely pay attention to the food as the conversation sets its own direction. We discuss kids, wives, schedules, and our work, its challenges and rewards. We do not try to convince each other of anything. We listen and respond without impediment; time and space evaporate. With elsewhere somewhere else, we focus on here, now, opening to each other fully and spontaneously. And as we return dirty dishes to the conveyor and stroll to the elevator, I realize the deepening of the bond between our spirits. We have met as *I* and *Thou*.

A year earlier, a minister friend and I took a group to Israel, with the hope that the thirty-five members of the church and the synagogue would explore their own religious roots while learning about each others'. The doctor and his wife joined our trip.

Late one chilly, cloudless winter afternoon, as the sun set behind the hills surrounding the Sea of Galilee, we boarded a small boat for a ride to Tiberias. Bundled against the wind and spray on the open deck, we huddled in small groups, chatting about the places we had visited and the places we were about to see. Of various faiths, we acknowledged our differences, respecting and cherishing them. Each of us held firm to our own faith and had no desire to get anyone else to change his or hers as we stood on that narrow ridge of a boat deck.

VOICES RISE
BETWEEN PEOPLE

I-Thou is in the voices we share—
from a simple chant to a grand opera.
I-Thou is not the silent voice within.

"Weddings must be fun," rabbis often hear, "and funerals must be awful." But the surprising truth is that the highs and lows of life are all the same. When the air vibrates with people, happily or sadly, a presence of *I-Thou* resonates.

In the days of the Hasidim, a young Jewish man became a master in a one-on-one apprenticeship with a mentoring master. So it happened that Leib, son of Sarah, learned all that the teachers of his home town, Rovno, could offer. Leib set out for Mezritch to continue study with a new master, Rabbi Dov Baer. When Leib returned to Rovno, curious townspeople asked him what new wisdom Rabbi Dov Baer had to share. Leib replied that he did not go to the Rabbi "to hear Torah from him but to see how he unlaces his felt shoes and laces them up again."[2] Whether Rabbi Dov Baer adjusted his shoes alone or whether Leib was with him, the lace and the knot were the same. But when Leib watched Rabbi Dov Baer, the aura of *I-Thou* embraced both men. There was something in the air in Mezritch—a gentle, ephemeral presence transforming an ordinary task into a religious occasion.

In the *I-It* relationship, I am wrapped up in myself—paying for the repairs to the roof of my home with whatever money the teller put into my account at the bank. On the other hand, it is just as easy for an *I-It* relationship to be entirely wrapped up in the other—as a roofer, working on a customer's home seven days a week, to the exclusion of what goes on under his or her roof. But when we get to the *I-Thou,* we are consumed, neither with you nor with me, but with what goes on between us.

Every *I-Thou* encounter is of the same spiritual substance, even though each one is unique. Every encounter is composed of identical ephemeral stuff, whether the moment is mundane or a milestone. *I-Thou* is the essence of the biblical Ruth's pledge to Naomi, "Wherever you go, I will go,"[3] and in the lifelong wandering partnership of Abraham and Sarah. Whether in an argument that startles like a bolt of thunder or in a soothing conversation, when pitched disagreement influences the direction of world history or when quieter words and actions shape human and divine destiny, *I-Thou* is any honest exchange between people.

When I was in social work school, a professor described the counsel she offered a couple in a physically abusive relationship.

"I know sometimes I hurt you," said the young man to the young woman in the presence of the counselor/professor. "But I still love you."

"That's not enough," the professor was reported to have interjected. "You cannot love someone you hit. When you act in a hurtful way, your feelings of love do not count. I don't care what you feel. It's all in what you do."

My teacher summed up the essence of *I-Thou*: "Pay little attention to what I think; watch what I do and say." Rabbi Mendel of Kotzk said, "It is with our doing that we grasp."[4] "Feelings accompany ... love, but they do not constitute it....Feelings dwell in the [person] ... love is *between* I and *Thou*."[5] I may feel happy talking to you, and you may feel angry. These feelings accompany *I-Thou*, but they are not the essence of *I-Thou*. *I-Thou* is in social settings, actions, words, and gestures.

I-Thou is doing, speaking, listening, and touching. Not in the *I* or in the *Thou*, *I-Thou* is essentially the "–," the dash that connects two people. *I-Thou* is not in the facts we know or in the emotions we harbor. "It is not like the blood that circulates in you, but like the air in which you breathe."[6] *I-Thou* is in the over-the-fence chat with a neighbor, in the greeting between deli clerk and customer, and in the late-night talk with a friend that takes an unexpected and exciting turn. *I-Thou* rises in the once-in-a-lifetime moment as it appears in daily life, or in a simple "Yes" or "No" uttered with the whole soul.

In looks, not in books, *I-Thou* is also wordless. It exists in a glance, in a frown, or in the library clerk's wink that says, "Forget the nickel fine." Rabbi Israel of Rizhyn taught:

> If a person speaks in the spirit of truth and listens in the spirit of truth, one word is enough, for with one word the world can be uplifted.[7]

I-Thou is in the fulfillment of religious obligations, on a pilgrimage to a religious shrine, during communal worship, in private prayer, or during the performance of the proper ritual on the assigned hour of the appropriate day of the week. *I-Thou* is not merely the peak experience of a fortu-nate few who have cultivated a particular depth of the spirit. *I-Thou* abides in all sorts of occasions.

RISING VOICES
ARE TRANSCENDENT

The songs rise above hardship.

A disciple questioned Rabbi Hayyim of Krosno's fascination with a tightrope walker. The master responded:

> This man is risking his life, and I cannot say why. But I am quite sure that while he is walking the rope, he is not thinking of the fact that he is earning a hundred Gulden by what he is doing, for if he did, he would fall.[8]

Rabbi Hayyim's tightrope walker does not consider the money, prestige, or audience rating that comes from pacing across the rope. *I-Thou* is of the same rapt focus. I see only the next person and myself; nothing else counts. *I-Thou* can be so engrossing that people pay attention to little else, even pain!

In *I-It*, one thing is on the mind—like the cost of a new roof—and something else gets said, such as how nice the weather has been. But in *I-Thou*, thought and speech, unified, consume full attention. In the intense focus of *I-Thou* at a hospital bedside, a patient forgets an upcoming medical procedure and a hospital visitor forgets a deadline back at the office. Only the person in front of me counts; everything else is a distraction, avoided, on the to-do list for later. *I-Thou* almost makes the pain go away.

When I was once recovering from surgery, a friend came by the hospital to offer a *mi shebairach*, a traditional Jewish prayer for healing. As I listened to the chant of the ancient Hebrew words, I felt embraced by every Jew who, seeking comfort, had ever said this prayer. My friend's words filled me with the same healing that has blessed people of our faith for centuries. She helped me put my pain out of my mind while she prayed, and in those moments I rose above my sickness.

I-Thou siphons our attention from little aches and great discomfort, financial worries and life-threatening illness. What was a moment ago all consuming—a low bank balance or a life crisis—evaporates into the rapt focus of *I-Thou*.

RISING VOICES OBSCURE TIME, SPACE, AND CAUSE

The cadence and content
of the song rise beyond the constraints
of time, space, and cause.

I-It tracks time, measures space, and looks for cause. In *I-Thou*, where you are, where you came from, where you are going, and for how long do not matter. The free-flowing *I-Thou* happens anytime and anywhere.

During the encounter, there is no sense of elapsed time. "My God," you exclaim as it ends, "I didn't realize that our conversation went on that long." And *I-Thou* rises at unpredictable times; a person never knows when it will arrive. *I-It*, preoccupied with moving faster and getting there sooner, measures the day and counts how far you went. *I-Thou* feels eternal, as if you have always been in it and will remain there forever. An onlooker clocks *I-Thou* with a stopwatch; to the partners, duration—an hour or a flicker—is irrelevant. *I-Thou* is timeless.

In *I-It*, we expend much time in a battle for space, or in a race to cover it, but space is not an issue in *I-Thou*. *I-It* is of the yardstick and tape measure, but to *I-Thou*, in common or obscure places, "where" makes no difference. Unlike the mantra "location, location, location," Judaism, a portable religion, worships at no shrine in particular. In the same fashion, *I-Thou* is unconcerned with site on the map. Partners are oblivious to their surroundings; attention to furniture, room temperature, neighboring conversations, or background music falls by the wayside.

Of statistical analysis and diagnosis, the *I-It* relationship looks for causes. In the *I-Thou* relationship, a person does not pick apart remarks and responses. A meeting between *I* and *Thou* never tries to unearth what led a person to say this or how a person came to feel that. What's behind the words is outside the scope of *I-Thou*. *I-Thou* sparks for the oddest reasons, but what ignites the flame is of no consequence. How we arrived, why we came together, why partners choose particular words—or no words—and what the words "really" mean are beyond the parameters of *I-Thou*. Uninterested in cause or motive, *I-Thou* lives in the moment without questioning the moment.

Voices Rise
Here and Now

**There is uplift in today's song more
than there is in yesterday's chant
or in tomorrow's tune.**

As the Bible tells it, when Lot's wife looked back on the
destruction of the sinful cities of Sodom and Gomorrah,
she became a pillar of salt. Observing her experience, we
would do well to avoid reflecting on the past when we can
live *I-Thou* now.

    I-It ruminates over what was. *I-It*, of the future as well,
worries about what's to come. Of the parent who sacrifices
everything today for tomorrow, one master, known as the
Yehudi, said to his disciples:

> If any one of you is asked why you toil so on earth,
> you reply, "To bring up my child to study and serve
> God." And after the child is grown up, the child
> forgets why the father toiled on earth, and toils in
> turn, and if you ask why, will say: "I must bring up
> my child to be studious and do good works." And so

it goes on, you people, from generation to generation. But when will we get to see the right child?[9]

I-It relationships imply, "If you do this, then I'll do that."
But *I-Thou* is in the moment. The Right Child is here now.

Many admirers sought the source of Rabbi Moshe of
Kobryn's rapt attention. A disciple, Mendel of Kotzk, when
asked to describe the master's essence, replied, "Whatever he
happened to be doing at the moment."[10] It is this moment—
the one we are in right now—that interlaces with divinity.

Rising Voices: Unpredictable, Arriving by Grace, and Unique

I-It is the old song played by rote.
I-Thou improvises,
making up the music as we go along.

Observing the natural human desire to control the course of destiny, Rabbi Pinhas of Koretz said: "What you pursue, you don't get. But what you allow to grow slowly in its own way comes to you."[11] I cannot *decide* to enter *I-Thou;* *I-Thou* erupts spontaneously. In the unique reaction to fresh circumstances, *I-Thou* opens in its own time, charts its own direction, and closes without warning. *I-It* is scripted and scheduled; *I-Thou* arrives and departs unannounced.

Because *I-Thou* is potentially so sweet, a person may wish to fabricate it to enjoy it, but only *I-It* can be concocted as such. "The *Thou* meets me through grace—it is not found by seeking."[12] We can set the stage for *I-Thou* by arranging to meet at a particular time and place. The rest happens by itself. Nothing creates *I-Thou*, brings it on sooner, pushes it deeper, or makes it more enjoyable.

But as easily as we invite *I-Thou*, we can block it—for a few hours, for years, or for an entire lifetime. Rabbi Menahem Mendel of Kotzk, a ponderous soul, wondered about God's presence and concluded: "God dwells wherever a person lets God in."[13] A person can keep God out or let God in.

Each *I-Thou* is unique. Fresh to life and never here before, *I-Thou* is one of a kind. We may have an additional encounter, but the new meeting will be very different. *I-Thou* may return to this place, but as a different song. Each time is the first—and the last.

Rising Voices:
A Capella *and*
Accompanied

**Rising voices pre-empt all other sounds
yet acknowledge that the whole world sings.**

I-Thou excludes all else as it includes all else.

On one hand, *I-Thou* excludes. When my lunch companion and I joined for a meal in the hospital cafeteria, *I-Thou* ignored surroundings. We took seats at a table set off in the corner for privacy; we removed our plates and utensils from trays and started to eat. As we entered the conversation in earnest, we entered *I-Thou*, looking beyond the details. We enjoyed the food and drink. We shut out the conversations at nearby tables. The only reality that counted was in our words. The atmosphere helped make up the whole, but once the conversation opened, the details were not the main event. We do not forsake *I-It* to enter *I-Thou*; we transform *I-It* to serve *I-Thou's* purpose.

On the other hand, everything around us sets the stage for *I-Thou*, as *I-Thou* includes all. The patient the doctor saw before our lunch, the medical procedures performed, the diagnoses concluded, and the medication dispensed helped bring us together, even though those items do not come up in the conversation. As "everything is gathered up in the relation,"[14] "everything else can be only the background out of which it emerges."[15] Under the paradox of inclusion and exclusion, I-Thou includes its surroundings, just as it excludes them.

Imagine a picture on the wall of a museum. The frame, the canvas, the hook, and the wire on the back of the frame make possible the display of art yet are not actively considered when a viewer studies the artwork. The studs in the wall and the floor and ceiling joists are essential to the picture on display but do not enter the mind. I-Thou fills the awareness. Everything else exists in the light of I-Thou, even as we ignore all other distractions.

RISING VOICES
LEAVE AN AFTERGLOW

**The music ends, not yet;
it continues to have an influence.**

Whether *I-Thou* is pitched—evoking stomach wobbles, arm
tingles, or the buckling of knees culminating in over-
whelming bliss—or rises calmly and peacefully like a full
moon on a clear night, we recognize *I-Thou* by its wake.

When Moses descended Mount Sinai with the Ten
Commandments in his arms, an aura surrounded him, sig-
nifying that his soul had changed through the encounter
with God. A person "does not pass, from moments of
the supreme meeting, the same being as he entered
into it …. something happens to the [person]."[16] In the
same fashion, after a candle's flame consumes a wick, a
wisp of smoke says, "A light was here." Like that aura
around Moses when he descended from Mount Sinai, like
that thin band of smoke, the afterglow is the most visible
sign of *I-Thou*, evident only once the encounter concludes.

When *I-Thou* ends, the afterglow does not come as
would a prize for winning a debate. We do not witness the

afterglow in the "gotcha" of clinching a deal. *I-Thou* is apparent in the reflection, "I learned something new about you and about me." Calmness, unease, happiness, melancholy, or even anger remains as the signature of *I-Thou*. A mood shift, coming from no word or gesture in particular but from the encounter as a whole, says, "Life has changed," not necessarily in a long-lasting or dramatic way but in an obvious one.

Once *I-Thou* concludes, we return to the daily grind accompanied by an energy boost or a perked-up feeling, by a sense of having met. Trivial matters that seemed important before the encounter now sit in proper perspective. And a person looks forward to the next encounter. A renewed spirit can mark the afterglow of *I-Thou*.

With the close of the academic year in Jerusalem, I returned to New York on a twelve-hour nonstop flight. Buber's *Tales of the Hasidim: The Later Masters*, traveling by sea, arrived eight weeks later. Not long after, I bought the companion volume, *The Early Masters*, this time paying full price—and I still got more than my money's worth.

At first, I found intimacy and peace in the stories and in *I-Thou*. As I continued to be mentored into the rabbinate, I discovered *I-Thou* in intense moments—in challenge, disappointment, and frustration. *I-Thou* is not always the happy romp through the sweet fields of life, as I soon learned from living and from returning to the old book.

PART FOUR

I-Thou on the Narrow Ridge

RISK

[T]he moments of *Thou* appear
as strange lyric and dramatic episodes,
seductive and magical,
but tearing us away
to dangerous extremes,
loosening the well-tried context,
leaving more questions than satisfaction
behind them, shattering security.[1]

At the office, 2:10 P.M.
I officiate at five or six wedding ceremonies a year.
Whether it's a first marriage or a second, a couple in their
twenties or in their sixties, we sit down to go over the
details of the ceremony: marriage canopy, family wine cup,
music, state license, and the like. Then I ask a few personal questions. "How did you meet?" "When did you decide
to get married?" "What convinced you?" To the last question, each couple invariably searches but only comes up
with "It just felt right." They instinctively realize how
hard it is to define *I-Thou*.

But something was different about one couple in their early thirties. It was a first marriage for both. In comparison with other couples, there seemed to be a listlessness between them, a lack of deep connection, a shortfall of romance. Was it me? Did I say something wrong? They answered all my questions fully, but I also felt that they were withholding something. I recalled hearing a little strain in the bride's voice when we made the appointment, as if she had then been about to tell me something but decided against it.

"Have your families met?" I asked, as I usually do. And now the feeling broke into the open.

"That is the big problem," said the groom. "My parents are divorced. My dad ran off with a younger woman a couple of years ago. He insists that she come to the wedding with him, or he doesn't come at all. If my dad comes, my mom stays home. Those are her conditions."

The bride started to cry. He took her hand, and she cried even harder.

"To hell with both of them," she said. "You ought to be more assertive."

"You always pick on them—and on me," he replied.

I cringed. "This is pretty painful." They offered a few more details. I suggested, "We could think about the possibility of my speaking to them."

"Maybe that will help. The two of us have to talk about it."

We chatted for a little while longer, until they began to pick up papers and coats, making it all too clear that they wanted to leave. We made another appointment for the following week. Within a few minutes, they were out of my study, leaving me to wonder about our conversation, whether I could have done something else, whether they would get married at all.

On one hand, something clicked. I saw less affection than I usually witness, but I also saw the bond of I-Thou when they said they had decided to marry because it "felt right." There is no better way to describe I-Thou. On the other hand, his parents were attempting to use them as pawns, as tools to their own agendas, as vehicles to express their anger to each other. The couple's communication problem with his parents and between the two of them bespoke a burgeoning I-It, a convoluted maze of envy, hurt, and rage that threatened to drive the couple apart. In this I-It world of "You listen to me, not to them," people become obstacles to the fullness of relation.

MISMEETING, BLURRING, OSCILLATION, AND ENRICHMENT

Voices clash as each sings
his or her song without attending
to the tune of the other.
Yet, rising voices intertwine—
rising, waning, and rising again—
strengthening each other.

The *I-It* of my wedding couple's conversation bespoke Mismeeting. No matter whether there is silence or speech in an exchange marked by Mismeeting, there is absolutely no communication.

It might be tempting to parse out this couple's conversation on a grid of *I-Thou/I-It*, but it would not be easy and might, in fact, be impossible. The distinction between *I-Thou* and *I-It* is often unclear. Whether we are enraged or exhilarated, there is a continuum, a blurring between the two, not a firm difference. Additionally, the couple, like anyone in conversation, flip-flopped between *I-Thou* encounter and *I-It* experience.

Many years after Martin Buber's mother left, he saw her again. It is hard to imagine the anticipation that must have filled both of their souls as they prepared for that reunion. As Buber described it, they tried to chat, but found they had nothing to say. Buber later remarked that this was an example of a Mismeeting in *I-It*, when words falter and fade away, when people fail to come together in *I-Thou*.

Have you ever tried to talk with a stranger—on a blind date or one-on-one with a business associate—but could not find the words? We mismeet in relatively superficial and trivial conditions as well as in crucial ones. When we mismeet, I can run only one side—my side—of the dialogue. I cannot take responsibility for both sides of a conversation: "We only know our part of the way, not"[2] the way of the other person. But Mismeeting does not mean that *I-Thou* is gone forever.

Ideally, we would live continuously and exclusively in *I-Thou* encounters, but this is impossible. Inevitably, *I-Thou* must yield to *I-It*. Hopefully, *I-Thou* returns. As *I-Thou* and *I-It* relations oscillate, one enriches the other.

Shifting between *I-It* and *I-Thou* strengthens both relations, as when a person goes beyond a job description. A teller can reach over the bank counter, not in body but with words, and with a simple but wholehearted "Thank you!" bring *I-Thou* into *I-It*. Life is fuller when a doctor and a patient speak to each other as people and when a boss treats workers not as mere hired help. Any good sales-person would rather have a sale rise out of a relationship than out of a sales pitch.

The *I-Thou* encounter infuses the *I-It* experience with spirituality. The *I-It* experience sets the stage for the *I-Thou* encounter. Rabbi Yitzhak of Vorki complimented an innkeeper who went out of his way to please his guests:

> "But he gets paid for it," someone remarked.
> "He accepts money," answered the Master, "so that it may be possible for him to fulfill the command-ment."[3]

A better innkeeper because of his humanity, and a better human being because of how he treats his guests! *I-Thou* and *I-It* support each other.

THE NARROW RIDGE

We sing on the Narrow Ridge.

The Narrow Ridge is any common ground, any sign of agreement, usually over the topic of discussion. People do not need to share the same opinion. They just have to agree on what to discuss. Sometimes, though, even that little bit of agreement is too much to achieve.

When it came to the meeting of *I* and *Thou*, Rabbi Moshe Leib of Sasov said:

> The way in this world is like the edge of a blade.
> On this side is the netherworld, and on that side is
> the netherworld, and the way of life lies in
> between.[4]

In this world, whether we sit with old friends over lunch or make new acquaintances, we encounter each other atop a slim Narrow Ridge—one that is no wider than the edge of a knife.

An example helps explain the Narrow Ridge. When flying in an airplane high above the ground, try sometime gazing out the window at trees, grass, and farms blanketing a valley. Viewed from high above, the valley rises gracefully and silently, until one valley meets another along a summit crest at the peak line. As valleys meet at the summit crest, *I* meets *Thou* on a Narrow Ridge between people.

Miles of contoured personality—acres and acres of life history—rest behind the peak line. When that bride and groom spoke respectfully and fully, without jealousy or fin-ger pointing, an opening of their personalities said "*I-Thou*," revealing just a little of their relationship. In *I-Thou*, only a small portion of one person needs to meet another person on that sliver of common ground known as the Narrow Ridge. But a person can fall from the Narrow Ridge as easily as slipping off the edge of a knife blade.

GROWING INTO *I-THOU*

I-Thou is about standing firm, holding one's
ground, even under personal attack.
Bit by bit, I came to understand
the importance of knowing oneself
and keeping to one's position in *I-Thou*.
My spirit got stronger, more independent,
with each *I-Thou* I entered.

Continuing my rabbinic studies in New York, I accepted an invitation to join the chaplain's staff at Manhattan's Memorial Sloan-Kettering Cancer Center. As a chaplain and student rabbi, I would visit Jewish patients—strangers—and offer what help I could.

Just anticipating the new job upset me. It led me to recall distant and unspoken fears, memories of my father's death and the deaths of others I loved. In nightmares, I saw myself on life-support systems like those I saw on the chaplain's orientation. Several nights in a row, I woke in the dark, gasping for air.

In more settled moments, I worried about saying something stupid to a patient. Just a student rabbi, a year out of college, I could conjugate any Hebrew verb and read a Hebrew newspaper. As a college psychology major, I could explain and critique Sigmund Freud's innovations. But when it came to advising someone with a life-threatening illness, my classmates and I believed we had little to offer.

Our supervisors understood our anxieties—probably from their own experience—and encouraged us to be natural and to feel free to ask for help. As for starting a conversation with a patient, we were told, "Introduce yourself by name as a student rabbi and a hospital chaplain and ask, 'How are you doing today?' Don't be frightened about saying something 'wrong.' Most people will forgive you."

It sounded simple enough, and to my surprise, it was simple at first. The people, though sick, were like everyone else. They were happy to have friendly visitors listen to their stories and reflections. These pleasant encounters showed me the healing power of relationships, even between strangers. But my real learning came a little later.

On the second day, I introduced myself to a patient and offered a chipper "How are you doing today?"

"What kind of jerk are you?" replied the man, in a bitter tone. "I am in a cancer hospital. How the hell should I feel?"

Shocked, I apologized for upsetting him. The man waved me off, and I left.

Later that day, a young woman gave me a similar response: "I don't need your help."

I was devastated. The two negative experiences pointed to my inadequacy. At the end of the day, I reviewed these conversations with a supervisor.

"That's what happens here," he offered. "Go see them again next week, unless they or someone else tells you never to come back. You have nothing to lose, only to gain. The worst they will do is throw you out again. You see, a person facing cancer is like a person facing anything else in life. And by coming here, you will firm up your personality, develop your sense of self, identifying what you believe and where you stand."

On subsequent visits, the man offered a tearful apology and shared his dread over his future. The young woman asked me to leave and to never return.

These experiences—the positive ones and the painful ones—were great teachers. Buber wrote, "Through the *Thou* a [person] becomes *I*."[5] It was not easy for me to become an *I*. But by talking to people in life-threatening situations, I became a richer, fuller, and stronger human being. I was afraid each time I walked into a patient's room. Nevertheless, every one of those difficult conversations taught me critical lessons about communication and living. I learned I cannot predict what I will hear and that I cannot be responsible for someone else's words. I learned to take responsibility for my words, to stand tall and hold my ground, never to cower, even in the face of another person's rage. I took comfort when people forgave my mistakes. Encounter after encounter, challenging ones and sweet ones, helped shape my spirit. By meeting people, I groomed and strengthened the adult within me.

OVER AND AGAINST

**Sweet music rises
when we sing the same note.
When different notes harmonize, however,
an additional dimension enters the song.**

Buber lived in the company of many friends and professional intimates. In 1922, Buber's close colleague, Franz
Rosenzweig, then aged thirty-five, was diagnosed with a
gradually declining terminal neurological condition.
Rosenzweig's doctors predicted that he would live a year.
By strength of spirit and with the support of family and
friends, he carried on for almost another decade.

No stranger to life's challenges, Rosenzweig had once
before interrupted his academic career for armed service in
Germany during World War I. Struck with inspiration for
writing what became the Jewish philosophy classic *The Star
of Redemption*, Rosenzweig mailed notes home from the
Balkan Front and completed the work after the war.

While in decline, Rosenzweig was embraced by his circle
of friends, including Buber, who conducted bedside prayer
services on Sabbaths and holidays. In failing health,
Rosenzweig nevertheless continued writing essays and ar-
ticles by hand until he became unable to handle a pen. His

wife took dictation until he lost the ability to speak. Then she brought in a customized typewriter that Rosenzweig could operate with one finger.

In 1924, the Christian publisher Lambert Schneider suggested that Buber prepare a new modern German translation of the Bible. It was time; and Buber, with his command of Jewish Scripture and language, was the right person for this substantial task. An intrigued Buber accepted—contingent on Rosenzweig's assistance.

Two years after the terminal diagnosis, Buber raised the idea with Rosenzweig, who wanted to join the project but hesitated because he did not expect to live to witness its completion. Buber suggested that Rosenzweig consider starting and going as far as he could. After some thought, Rosenzweig agreed with enthusiasm, and the two began work immediately.

According to schedule, Buber prepared a first draft for Rosenzweig's review, finalizing the text during Buber's twice-weekly visits. By the end of 1925, they had completed Genesis. Within the next six months, they concluded Exodus. By Rosenzweig's death in 1929, the two had translated the five Books of the Pentateuch—that is, the Torah—as well as the Books of Joshua, Judges, and Kings: a significant section of the Bible. Buber finished the translation in Jerusalem in 1961.

Imagine two children gazing at the sky, picturing animal shapes in the random cloud formations. One points to a cloud and says it resembles a kitten. The other child sees a rabbit in the same cloud. Over and Against happens when we have different perceptions of the same thing. When both children see the identical beast in the air, they do not have much to discuss. When they see different animals and have the spiritual wherewithal to compare perspectives, then a conversation can flourish.

Over and Against is the healthy tension between people, an interpersonal challenge that creates an opportunity to reach a new opinion, a different worldview. We respect the approach of the other in Over and Against. We try to see the world through each other's eyes as we, at the same time, try to see it through our own.

Some people believe that spirituality occurs when people are united in opinion and purpose. Over and Against means that I stand in place, affirming my belief. "[M]eet others, and hold your ground when you meet them."[6] *Because* we do not see eye to eye, *because* we affirm our positions, we stand Over and Against.

When we agree all the time, there is no rough edge to the relationship, and there is no opportunity for growth. Without Over and Against, we are like tires spinning on the ice without gaining traction. There is no movement, no progress. If we merely and continually nod in agreement, we come away from each other exactly as we came together.

Buber and Rosenzweig stood Over and Against. They both knew that Rosenzweig had little time left. Whereas Buber believed his friend was up to the task, Rosenzweig, however, was reluctant to begin. Their differences in perception offered them an opportunity to discuss the issues. There was no stubbornness within either man, only a willingness to dialogue. Perhaps Rosenzweig was hesitant to start something he could not finish. Perhaps Rosenzweig thought he could not carry a fair share of the responsibility; he did not want to be a burden to Buber or disappoint him. Yet, Buber's behavior suggested, "I would like you to start this. At least begin the task with me. I cherish whatever contribution you offer." Thus, Rosenzweig came around and said, "Yes." It is in Over and Against, in our differences, that our conversations can bring the greatest spiritual growth.

Buber used the term *Confirmation* to describe the spiritual growth achieved in the wake of Over and Against. It is similar to the psychological term *unconditional positive regard*, an unqualified faith in the worth of the individual. As I display unconditional positive regard for you, I emphasize a deep affirmation of your dignity and goodness. Confirmation is unconditional positive regard—and more. Added to that unwavering high respect, Confirmation says that we accept each other *and* that we challenge each other to grow.

When Buber, in Confirmation, introduced Rosenzweig to the notion of cooperating on a translation, Rosenzweig responded with uncertainty. A third person, an onlooker, might have predicted that one of the two men would come away from the conversation with a different opinion. In the dialogue that followed, both men put it on the line. As it turned out, Buber *confirmed* Rosenzweig into the growth he envisioned.

THE NEW THINKING

Each time we meet, we sing a novel tune.
The New Thinking is not
a rote chant of a worn-out melody
but a new song for a new moment.

In earlier, healthier years, Rosenzweig's term *New Thinking* described novel ideas that come to life in a conversation. Out of an encounter with Buber, Rosenzweig discovered and embraced an innovative idea—working on a translation despite his illness.

I don't learn much from *I-It* experiences. The teller reports on my new bank balance, and the roofer helps me understand the fine points of shingles. I am happy to know these new facts. But the knowledge I gain from *I-Thou* touches my spirit much more deeply.

The New Thinking rises on the Narrow Ridge. When God spoke at the summit crest of Mount Sinai, that speech gave the People of Israel the innovative concepts of the Torah. In the same fashion, the communication of New Thinking brings a new self-awareness. "See how I reacted when he said that to me!" is one example. "Look at what I did when that woman challenged my statement!" is another.

With a new self-perspective, I see myself in a new situation with new eyes.

As a little boy, Buber was confirmed by his grandparents. They accepted his goodness and, through words and deeds, led him to the New Thinking. His grandparents set out goals for him: to learn and experience, to enter the world, not as a broken soul but as a productive member of society. Their attitude toward Martin reassured him, confirmed him as a good and capable individual who was worthy of their support and would honor their trust. The New Thinking of self-image grew out of the deep bond between Martin and his grandparents.

IMAGINE THE REAL

We focus on the melody
coming from our partner
while carefully attending to our own song.

I-Thou reaches across the Narrow Ridge to Imagine the
Real.

To Imagine the Real, put your hand on my arm. Feel me
in your hand, and wonder what your hand feels like to me.
To Imagine the Real is to touch and imagine being
touched, to be aware of one's health while inferring another's pain. To Imagine the Real, look into the eye and wonder about the soul, all the while keeping in touch with the
self. In a mental picture that rises all by itself, partners
fathom the full range of the relationship from both sides
simultaneously. But we cannot know the full truth of the
other. We can only imagine.

After World War I, Buber's close friend Gustav Landauer,
a political activist, was imprisoned for his ideas and actions
and beaten to death by his captors. Landauer's murder was a
great spiritual shock to Buber, who knew his friend was
innocent of any crime. When Buber first got the news of
Landauer's horrible fate, he could not grasp the facts; the
image strained the limit of his comprehension. Buber tor-

mented himself with his attempts to imagine how Landauer had taken those blows, what Landauer had made of his situation as he began to lose consciousness. In later years, Buber remarked how hard it was to Imagine the Real. He seemed to have made peace with Rosenzweig's illness: a biological injustice. But Landauer's murder, a social evil, afflicted Buber with continuing emotional torment and pointed to the limits of living the full experience of another person.

To Imagine the Real is to suppose the contours of an unknown spiritual landscape. As Rabbi Mordechai of Nezchizh remarked to his son, the Rabbi of Kovel:

> One who does not feel the pains of a woman giving birth within a circuit of fifty miles, who does not suffer with her and pray that her suffering be assuaged is not worthy to be called a *zaddik* [a master].[7]

Rabbi Mordechai wanted his son to imagine a common and intense experience—giving birth—that he would never experience himself. By the same token, the engaged couple I mentioned earlier needed to make the effort to know each other's hearts, all the while coming to grips with the secrets within their own. As we come to Imagine the Real of our partner, we come closer to becoming the master under the spiritual mentorship of Rabbi Mordechai of Nezchizh.

When we are able to Imagine the Real, we take an important step toward Confirmation. When we try to see each other as we are, we are ready to take the next step, well prepared to begin to see each other in terms of what we can become.

Mutuality is at heart when we Imagine the Real and undertake Confirmation. *I-Thou* is reciprocal. I have the right to attempt to change you, but only if I am willing to risk being changed by you. I accept and love you, but I also love and respect what you can become. We teach each other; we prompt, motivate, and support each other's effort to rise to challenge, to fulfill the responsibilities life calls us to address.

COMMUNITY, STRIFE, AND HOLY INSECURITY

Rising voices carry across the globe.

I-Thou expands well beyond the two of us, well past the cafeteria lunch conversation and the words between cloud-gazing children. From his childhood experience with Hasidism, Buber learned of the importance of community, where members are open, honest, and spiritually intimate with each other.

Instead of knitting together as a community, we all too often withdraw from one another. I grew up in a big city, a place of faceless strangers, nameless customers, and color-less neighbors. In my large apartment house, I met many recognizable strangers whom I never greeted and who never greeted me. We passed in the hall while bringing out the trash. We waited together for the elevator, not even sharing a curt "Good morning." Our conversation never went deeper than our emotionless faces. We entered no depth of relation; our voices fell and remained silent in one another's presence.

Buber would want us to transform that group of isolated individuals into the linked lives of a cohesive community. Desiring more than a circle of one-to-one acquaintances, he encouraged us to extend our relationships to the larger community, an ethical community based on the principles of respect and dignity at the heart of the *I-Thou* encounter: social justice, economic parity, and political equality. Out of the model of the Hasidic community he saw as a child, Buber dreamed of a human harmony that reached even further, well beyond the local to the international. Buber held close the vision of a world human family composed of cooperative communities.

Buber was not a pacifist. Having lived in Europe during World War I, fled that homeland before the outbreak of World War II, and resided in strife-filled Israel from 1938 to 1965, he regretfully admitted that there are times when a nation must turn to military defense. Nevertheless, Buber hoped for warm peace, not the unstable peace that emerged from the Cold War. Under the shadow of nuclear mutual destruction, peace is shallow and fragile. A stronger and more enduring peace, he believed, can be established in a true encounter between adversaries.

Buber envisioned honesty and openness between world leaders. Heads of state and local elected officials too often sculpt their words to suit political purposes instead of ethical responsibilities. They set out not to create a dialogue but to intimidate their opponents abroad and strengthen their supporters at home. Having witnessed the horror and tragedy of armed strife, Buber recognized the instability of the human condition and the heartache of personal loss. Buber coined the term *Holy Insecurity* to speak of the fragility of the human being.

THE LAST ROW

**We sing one note and expect another
to follow, but will it?**

I-It is scripted. I walk up to the teller's counter, hand over
checks, and come away with a receipt. *I-Thou*, balanced on
the Narrow Ridge, takes a risk; it is about the unexpected.
Because *I-Thou* is filled with the unpredictability of Over
and Against, Confirmation, and New Thinking, I cannot
foretell what will come of it.

Rabbi Nahum of Stepinesht surprised his students,
catching them at checkers instead of at study. The morti-
fied students feared the master's anger.

> But he gave them a kindly nod and asked, "Do you
> know the rules of the game of checkers?" And
> when they did not reply for shyness he himself gave
> the answer: "I shall tell you the rules of the game of
> checkers. The first is that one must not make two
> moves at once. The second is that one may only
> move forward and not backward. And the third is
> that when one has reached the last row, one may
> move to where one wants."[8]

"One step at a time" and "forward, never back" are fine pieces of advice; that's life. But the last row, where one can allegedly act as one pleases, is something else.

One man dreams, "I'll be in the last row when I earn $30,000 a year more." Another says, "I'll reach my last row when I get that promotion." A young mother remarks, "My life will calm down when our youngest reaches full-day kindergarten." Everyone wants to get to a point of calmness and comfort, as if such a place really exists. Truth be told, there is no last row, just the Holy Insecurity of life, the ongoing confrontation with surprises and challenges, even disaster and disappointment.

Rabbi Nahum was teasing his students with the false security of the last row. He knew *I-Thou* as something over which "one never gains as an assured possession."[9] Like the horizon point where the train rails appear to meet, the last row is an optical illusion, a trick of the eye, a storybook "happily ever after" fantasy ending we never reach. We dream of a last row but never arrive—not with a promotion or after graduation, not when the kids leave for college, not in retirement or at the end of life.

After the Exodus from Egyptian slavery, free from Pharaoh, the Jewish people must have thought, "We have it made. We have nothing to worry about, ever." Rabbi Israel of Koznitz reminds us, "Every day, a person shall go forth out of Egypt, out of distress."[10] That is, getting out of the distress of Egypt—achieving redemption from darkness—is a lifelong struggle.

Maintaining an *I-Thou* relationship is an ongoing effort, not a final destination. *I-Thou* continues to live "only if a [person] realises God anew in the world according to [one's] strength and to the measure of each day."[11] It is a process, not a product; a risky way of living but the only honest life.

To enter *I-Thou* is to embrace Holy Insecurity, to accept an inescapable, sacred uncertainty. I take a chance. I risk saying the wrong thing or having my words met with rejection. At times, the Narrow Ridge offers a peaceful stroll along a quiet trail; at other times, the mountain hiker slogs through mud in uncharted territory. Too often, life is an obstacle course strewn with fallen branches, studded with rocks, and blocked by boulders. The *I-Thou* relationship is a rickety indicator of the truth; *I-Thou* wobbles with the same tremor seen in that mountain hiker's compass as it points to the north. The only security in *I-Thou* is in continually accepting the insecurity, making peace with the risk.

I-Thou, a spirituality of the rough and tumble, is the faith of Martin Buber. Although deserted by his mother, he was not distrustful but was always willing to trust anew. Unlike the woman who mistook Rabbi David of Lelov for her husband and reacted to an old wrong, Buber blamed no one for being abandoned. Instead, he accepted Holy Insecurity, entering new relationships, chancing the healing possibilities of *I-Thou*. As for the wedding couple I met in my office, their insecurity led me to wonder whether the wedding would take place at all, and I was left hanging until our next meeting.

Every person worries over something. Sharing that insecurity with another person makes all the difference. In *I-It*, we keep anxiety under wraps. In *I-Thou*, we remove the wrapper and reveal feelings. Holy Insecurity tore at Rabbi Hanoch's spirit. He finally found the strength to discuss his dark brooding with Rabbi Bunam, who replied,

"That's the same question I have carried around with me all my life. You will come and eat the evening meal with me today."[12]

All people carry sadness within. But there is comfort and security with the open heart of *I-Thou* when it intersects in the invisible spirituality of *Eternal Thou*. Now we can remove the hand from the eye entirely, revealing the holiness of those enormous lights and mysteries of *Eternal Thou*.

PART FIVE

Eternal Thou:
A Leap of Faith

Entering the Eternal

... grace, for which one must always be ready ...[1]

Dinner at temple, 6:55 P.M.

With the main course over and dessert coming out, I feel a tap on the shoulder and hear a whisper.

"Phone for you."

I weave between tables into the noisy kitchen.

The call is from a doctor at the hospital.

"I just left a patient. You don't know the person. He's very sick, says he has had enough suffering. He's tired of being a burden on his family, wants to disconnect all the equipment and just die. But before I do anything, I think he should talk to you. Could you stop by?"

There is nothing wrong with saying "I have had enough" when death nears, when no drug or medical procedure will significantly extend or enhance a person's days. But when a rabbi faces a question of life and death—a rabbi representing a life-affirming faith—he or she has an obligation to ask a few questions about the decision.

"I'll be over in a little bit."

One of our seminary teachers taught us that a rabbi must feel *something* with each funeral, wedding, and the like.

Otherwise, what's the point? After twenty years in the rabbinate, remnants of the feelings I knew during each of those intense pastoral experiences must be piling up in a hidden corner of my soul. It's an extra emotional weight I carry whenever I go to the hospital. But something more than that embedded tinge of trepidation is growing as I approach the hospital, more than some ensconced residue of two decades of compassionate listening.

After my appendectomy, my very first experience with surgery just a year ago, I woke from the anesthesia with an irritated throat made raw by tubes inserted and removed. I felt nauseated and depleted. With eyes half spinning, half shut under the bright light, I tried to figure out where I had been cut open. "Now roll to the left," I heard, not knowing why they were asking or why I was complying. "Now roll to the right." I eventually realized they were using a plastic board to move me from a bed to a gurney to return me to my room. But more than a memory of that three-day hospitalization nags at my spirit. More than the memory of my father's untimely death jolts the back of my mind. My thoughts turn to the image of my own end.

I know I will come back to the hospital one day, not to see someone else but for myself, because of my own frailty and mortality. Although I will be challenged and frightened and in pain, there will be comfort for me, God willing, even then. Although I will wander the dark woods, alone and lost, a nurse, a doctor, a technician, a family member, or a friend will join me on that Narrow Ridge. A voice will call out to me, and a hand will reach for mine to calm my trembling through *I-Thou*.

I-THOU:

DELICATE AND ETERNAL

[T]he radial lines that proceed
from all the points of the *I* to the Centre,
form a circle.[2]

I-Thou looks like a simple balance, as it often is. Yet, *I-Thou* calls so little attention to itself that we often ignore it; *I-Thou* arrives and departs unnoticed. The most well-meaning people, engrossed in the vital details of life, fail to recognize the soft-spoken *I-Thou*. Pressing daily responsibilities overtake religious subtlety, and sacred opportunities repeatedly pass unappreciated. All too sadly, *I-Thou* gets lost in the fray of schedules, deadlines, and appointments. The tender *I-Thou* is trampled in the rush for the train or drowned out by ringing phones and beeping fax machines and the tinkle of instant messages. When the door to *I-Thou* closes and locks by itself, life declines into Buber's second relationship: *I-It*.

Life is awful without *Thou*. Some people, because the spirit is weak, impaired, or under duress, never say *Thou*—ever. Dialogue fails when relatives or old friends have a

falling out and never talk again, or when contract negot-
iations collapse into a labor strike or a lockout, or when
diplomatic consultations break down and lead to war. We
cannot enter I-Thou with every person we meet. But a
master has the faith and skill needed to lower the hand
and raise the voice under any circumstances.

As Rabbi Hayyim of Zanz taught us, this world is like a
deep forest where each person wanders alone. Hearing a
voice in the distance, I lift my voice and call out in the
dark. A voice calls back. Hand reaches for hand, and voice
lifts voice in I-Thou. These quiet triumphs of the spirit
never make the newspaper headlines. But they make the
world a better place and leave a permanent impact in
Eternal Thou. "[I]n each Thou we address the Eternal
Thou,"[3] said Martin Buber. As we converse with each
other, we also speak to God in the Eternal Thou.

I find the doctor at the nurses' station. We enter the patient's
room together. I meet a very sweet, elderly gentleman.

"Why don't you tell me a little about your life?" I suggest.

In a voice grown nearly inaudible by illness and treat-
ments, the man in the bed begins to describe a simple
childhood in Brooklyn, New York. With the noisy beeps
and whooshing of the hospital machines, I have to put my
ear to his mouth to hear about college, marriage, building
up a business, two kids, and beautiful grandchildren. His
wife of fifty-one years died a few months earlier.

Then we get to here and now. After twenty years of
struggling with cancer and heart disease, he says, without
anger or remorse, that he believes his continued suffering
accomplishes nothing. Doctors give him no more than a
couple of months. It's time to stop being a burden on

everyone. His family wants nothing of this plan; they want him to live as long as possible. They also know that the patient's word rules. And the doctor, worried that the man is going too soon, wants him to talk with me before coming to a firm decision.

ALL LIVING IS MEETING

... spoken with the whole being ...[4]

By now it's clear that my conversation with the terminally ill patient was not strictly an *I-Thou* encounter. I am the rabbi, and the man in the bed seeks my professional opinion. It's *I-It*. But in the presence of a full life and imminent death, I feel a little like that uncertain second-year rabbinic student. Death is an equalizer. Humbled by the man's calmness, realism, and candor, all I can say is *Thou*.

The man is too vibrant. It *is* too soon. He offers the world "nothing"? He puts his honest feelings on the line, and I feel obligated to offer mine. The illness is just physical; his spirit is strong.

"No matter what you decide to do," I say, "I will carry the memory of this moment with me for a very long time."

He smiles. "I am flattered." I breathe, feeling a little relief.

"I don't want your life to end before it has to," I continue. "You are in pain now, but I believe you would be willing to bear even greater pain if you had a reason to do so. So this conversation is really not about suffering—yours or your family's. It is about identifying a reason to continue living. I suggest that this is the reason: to continue to talk to other people the way you are talking to me. You have a wonderful influence on your caregivers, on me, and on your family. You have a purpose in life. By talking, by sharing perceptions, you can continue to make a difference to the world. And let me also add that I don't get to talk to too many people like this."

He is visibly moved by my words. We chat a little longer: the man, the doctor, and me. I offer to return for another visit; he says he will have someone call if he wants one. In less than an hour, I am back at temple and involved in other things. But in the days that follow, the man is on my mind.

A month later, a son calls with the news of his father's death.

ETERNAL THOU

**Every particular *Thou* is
a glimpse through to the *Eternal Thou*.** [5]

Our meeting touched a sick man, a doctor, and a rabbi in *I-Thou*. Moreover, each time we said "Thou" our words resonated in *Eternal Thou*, that invisible heavenly repository. To better Imagine the Real of the *Eternal Thou*, let us return to Rabbi Abraham Yaakov of Sadgora—to his trains, phones, and telegraphs—for some New Thinking. When Rabbi Abraham Yaakov remarked, "They hear there what we say here," he had in mind a person speaking and a person listening. And I believe that he had in mind much more. Write "there" as "There," with a capital T. What we say "here" is also heard "There," by the Divine Listener, who gathers in all words and deeds for eternity.

Imagine Rabbi Abraham Yaakov at the train station. He arrives early, for he knows that by one second he could well miss it all. He stands between the tracks and gazes into the distance, hoping to get a first glimpse of the arriving train. As the tracks approach the horizon he notes that, thanks to a trick of the eye, the rails appear to converge. Then he mulls over the reality that *I* meets *Thou* in the narrow spaces, between the rails of life.

When *I* meets *Thou*, it seems that people converge, but Rabbi Abraham Yaakov knew to shun "the feeling of a unity that does not and cannot exist."[6] Two people do not become one in *I-Thou*; that is just another optical illusion. Each person remains distinct and independent. But in *Eternal Thou*, beyond our sight and over the horizon, there is an invisible intersection of every *I-Thou* with God.

I meets *Thou* at the bank and over lunch, on the pulpit and at a hospital bedside. By now, it seems that *I-Thou* is relatively easy to recognize and explain: lift voices, join hands, and there it is. With *Eternal Thou*, we cannot see. All we can do is Imagine the Real. *I-Thou* on earth bestows an invisible but permanent heavenly impact in *Eternal Thou*. *Eternal Thou* is not a matter of fact but an article of faith.

ETERNAL THOU:
JEWISH ROOTS

... who speaks the word God
and really has *Thou* in mind ...[7]

Buber is called a Jewish existentialist because he addresses
the conditions of human life from a Jewish perspective.
The lessons I have tried to convey in this book speak to
the lives of people of all faiths, but they are based on
Judaism, drawing from biblical and mystical sources.

I-Thou, I-It, and *Eternal Thou* reflect the traditional
Jewish themes of Creation, Revelation, and Redemption.
According to Jewish thought, in Creation God formed the
universe, in Revelation God gave the Torah, and in
Redemption God freed the People of Israel from bondage
in Egypt, foreshadowing the eventual redemption of all
humanity from hardship.

In the Bible's story of Creation, God commanded, "Let
there be light," and the world came to be. We also create in
I-Thou, through our speech, through each unique, spoken
word. God's Revelation made known a new religious truth.
When *I* meets *Thou* in New Thinking, we discover a new
teaching, as holy as any word from God or as any sacred

literature. By taking the lessons of Revelation and applying them to God's Creation, we bring the universe closer to Redemption. As God redeemed Israel from slavery in Egypt, we follow God's example and attempt to bring freedom from suffering and heartache through *I-Thou.*

Speaking of redemption, Martin Buber often turned to the Psalms of Jewish Scripture. He read Psalm 73 at Franz Rosenzweig's funeral and had it recited at his own burial and inscribed on his grave marker:

> I am with You always;
> You hold my right hand.
> Guide me with Your counsel,
> And after take me in glory.
> Who have I in the heavens?
> And with You, I need nothing on earth.[8]

As we place our hands in each other's, we also join hands with God, who gathers us in glory through *I-Thou* in *Eternal Thou* forever. As Rabbi Aaron of Karlin said, when a person "stands solidly on the earth, then that person's head reaches up to Heaven."[9] This is *Eternal Thou.*

THE JEWISH
MYSTICAL TRADITION

**... where the extended lines of relations
meet—in the *Eternal Thou*.[10]**

Tales of the Hasidim was originally published in Hebrew
under the name of *Or Haganuz* ("The Hidden Light"). One
Hasidic story, "The Hidden Light," appears in the Hebrew
edition on the back cover but is absent from the English
translation. The omitted story describes a primordial light,
a light appearing at Creation, very different from the sun-
light or electric light we know:

> Rabbi Eliezer said: "In the light that God created
> on the first day, a person could see from one end of
> the world to the other. When God foresaw the mis-
> deeds of future generations, God hid this light from
> them, reserving it for the righteous of the future."
> Asked the disciples, "Where was it hidden?" He
> replied, "In the Torah...." They asked, "If so, what
> should the righteous do when they find some of
> this hidden light in the Torah?" He replied, "They
> should reveal it in the way they live."[11]

Although the primordial light remains hidden, Rabbi Eliezer's disciples had the means to bask in its radiance as we do. According to the mystics, each time we do a mitz-vah—fulfill a religious obligation—we reclaim a splintered ember of this original brilliance. Honoring the teachings of the sacred text, visiting the sick, celebrating a marriage, observing the Sabbath and holidays, or traveling to Israel—these are all ways to join hands and voices in *I-Thou* and enter the *Eternal Thou*.

These are the Jewish roots of *Eternal Thou*. To Imagine the Real in *Eternal Thou* is to fathom how earthly deeds influence an invisible heavenly counterpart, and how that Divine Partner affects us. To stand on a Narrow Ridge in Holy Insecurity is to risk restoring—or losing—the hidden light. According to Rabbi Shalom Sachna of Probitz, we are able "to let the hidden life of God shine out in this lowest world,"[12] illuminating one end of the universe to the other. In the trivial and in the monumental, each *I-Thou* intersects with *Eternal Thou* in that invisible spiritual storehouse where all our doings are gathered forever.

URGENCY

You know always in your heart
that you need God more than everything;
but do you not know too
that God needs you...?[13]

God exists thanks to our righteous acts and their heavenly influence. God longs to embrace our goodness. But we have limited opportunity to exert this divine impact.

The most productive periods of Buber's life were the times when he feared his career was ending: before he fled Germany and before his death. Expecting a door to close on his days, he worked his hardest to make the most of the time remaining. God needs us to exert ourselves as Buber did, to make the greatest possible and positive impact on the *Eternal Thou* in this short lifetime.

Buber wants us to approach life with Rosenzweig's passion, the undaunted tenacity to fight against a deadline, to complete as much as possible. Any missed opportunity to enter *I-Thou*—with a stranger or with an intimate—leaves emptiness in the *Eternal Thou* forever. There is just one life, one chance to abide with God. When an opportunity to approach God is squandered, the opportunity to make a permanent difference is lost. Our chances are limited in number and duration, and our time on earth is measured. Between the rising and setting of each day's sun, we need to strive to transform ordinary moments into religious occasions as *I* meets *Thou* in the *Eternal Thou*.

BECOMING THE MASTER

> You need God, in order to be—
> and God needs you.[14]

We may never reach the promised last row, but a master always heads in that direction. And how will the master travel? Merely concerned with riding a better wagon and dressing in a better coat? No matter what the master wears, regardless of the master's destination, the means of travel, or the itinerary, the master rides with good companions in relation. So, let the phone ring, let the telegraph continue clacking, and let the trains travel through the night. The master will raise her voice and join hands in *I-Thou*.

While lacing a boot or when facing death, the master's voice rises with yours. Those two voices find yet another voice and raise that one as well. So board a train as a master, knowing that the fellow commuter is not an *It* but a *Thou*. Answer the phone as a master, remembering that a person is on the line, not just a problem. And send that cable, fax, or e-mail as a master, because a human being will read it. Only when we act in this fashion will we meet—on daily errands, in the aftermath of a personal crisis, or during a national trauma. As Rabbi Israel of Koznitz said, "With one look, one can gain the coming world"[15] in *Eternal Thou*. There we will encounter God in the last row, where the rails really do meet, in *Eternal Thou*, where God needs us.

Sometimes the last row appears beyond reach. In Planet Hospital, in a rabbi's study, or at the bank, it looks as if the rails will never meet and no voice will ever rise. These are my most challenging moments: when the acting-out child refuses to listen, when the woman in spiritual crisis spurns an offer of assistance, or when the angry man asks me a question but tries to give me his answer rather than listen to my response. When people say *It* when they hear *Thou* because of a birthplace, shade of skin, or sexual orientation, we need the master. Hearing *It*, the master responds *Thou*. The master's faith says, "You will join hands with me."

EPILOGUE:
AT DAY'S END

He who loves a woman ...
is able to look in the _Thou_ of her eyes
into a beam of the _Eternal Thou_."[1]

At home, 10:05 P.M.

At this day's end—one a little longer and a little more intense than most—I sit down in the family room with my wife, Debbie, who is a rabbi like me with days like mine. Having arrived home earlier in the evening, she helped the kids with homework, saw them to bed, and now, on the couch, reads the newspaper and keeps an eye on one of those hospital TV shows. Against the backdrop of as much pretend blood, romance, rant, and rage between two commercials as I see in a week, we review the day's song, a few of the high notes and some low ones—all in *I-Thou.*

Our conversation flows to a discussion of the kids' day. With the approaching end of a school marking period, one of the kids has to make up missing homework assignments. A missed assignment leaves an empty space in the teacher's homework record, resulting in a lowered report card grade and an impact on the permanent school record.

I rub my tired eyes during a commercial break. My mind flows to the higher permanent record, God's roll book of lost opportunities and captured promises, to the eternal dwelling place of all the good that a person ever achieves.

As Debbie and I talk on, I recall my words with the bank teller, the tap on the shoulder for the hospital call, that bedside discussion of life and death, and the hardship of the couple contemplating marriage. Not all of my reflections enter the conversation, but I am sure that what I did goes toward that invisible permanent record. It was a day of *I-It,* from the bank to the roof. But it is only the *I-Thou* that is gathered in for good.

As I prepare for bed and drift off to sleep, I recall my own school days. When the school year reached spring, I often turned back in my loose-leaf notebook to the class notes I took in the early fall. By spring, I had forgotten what I learned in the fall—until the notes reminded me. Just the same, all life's lessons are kept somewhere—all the earthly goodness, what of life is remembered, and what is forgotten. All is recorded in the invisible notebook, abiding with God, in the permanent repository we call *Eternal Thou.*

Notes

Preface

1. Martin Buber, *I and Thou*, trans. Ronald Gregor Smith (New York: Scribner Classics, 1986), 19.

2. Genesis 28:16.

Introduction

1. *I and Thou*, 59.

2. *I and Thou*, 67.

3. "One Small Hand," in Martin Buber, *Tales of the Hasidim: Early Masters*, trans. Olga Marx (New York: Schocken Books, 1975), 74.

4. "Looking for the Way," in Martin Buber, *Tales of the Hasidim: Later Masters*, trans. Olga Marx (New York: Schocken Books, 1975), 213.

Part One—Our Daily Encounters

1. *I and Thou*, 51.

2. *I and Thou*, 40.

3. *I and Thou*, 50.

4. *I and Thou*, 58.

5. *I and Thou*, 105.

6. *I and Thou*, 31.

7. *I and Thou*, 30–1.

8. *I and Thou*, 95.

9. "Angels and Humans," in *Later Masters*, 161.

10. *I and Thou*, 122–3.

11. *I and Thou*, 71.

Part Two—*I-It:* A Spirit in Eclipse—Seven Stories

1. *I and Thou,* 54.
2. *I and Thou,* 60–1.
3. "Of Modern Inventions," in *Later Masters,* 70.
4. "In a Hurry," in *Early Masters,* 226.
5. *I and Thou,* 52.
6. *I and Thou,* 47.
7. "Roads," in *Later Masters,* 134.
8. *I and Thou,* 44.
9. "The Darkness of the Soul," in *Later Masters,* 308.
10. "Everyone Has a Place," in *Later Masters,* 72.
11. "The Horses," in *Early Masters,* 240.
12. "Depending on God," in *Later Masters,* 92.
13. "A Vain Search," in *Later Masters,* 314.
14. "The Mistake," in *Later Masters,* 186.
15. "The Real Exile," in *Later Masters,* 315.
16. "When Two Sing," in *Early Masters,* 126.

Part Three—*I-Thou:* When One Voice Lifts Another

1. *I and Thou,* 26.
2. "To Say Torah and to Be Torah," in *Early Masters,* 107.
3. Ruth 1:16.
4. "The Vessel," in *Later Masters,* 277–8.
5. *I and Thou,* 28–9.
6. *I and Thou,* 49.
7. "The Word," in *Early Masters,* 236.
8. "The Rope Dancer," in *Early Masters,* 174.
9. "The Right Child," in *Later Masters,* 231.
10. "Most Important," in *Later Masters,* 173.
11. "What You Pursue," in *Early Masters,* 129.
12. *I and Thou,* 26.
13. "God's Dwelling," in *Later Masters,* 277.
14. *I and Thou,* 80.

15. *I and Thou*, 41.
16. *I and Thou*, 104.

Part Four—*I-Thou* on the Narrow Ridge

1. *I and Thou*, 44.
2. *I and Thou*, 78.
3. "Commandment and Money," in *Later Masters*, 295.
4. "The Way of Life," in *Later Masters*, 92.
5. *I and Thou*, 39.
6. *I and Thou*, 43.
7. "Get the Measure," in *Early Masters*, 164.
8. "Playing Checkers," in *Later Masters*, 73.
9. *I and Thou*, 121.
10. "Every Day," in *Early Masters*, 290.
11. *I and Thou*, 108.
12. "Master and Disciple," in *Later Masters*, 251.

Part Five—*Eternal Thou:* A Leap of Faith

1. *I and Thou*, 121.
2. *I and Thou*, 108.
3. *I and Thou*, 22.
4. *I and Thou*, 25.
5. *I and Thou*, 77.
6. *I and Thou*, 87.
7. *I and Thou*, 77.
8. Psalm 73:23–25.
9. "On the Earth," in *Early Masters*, 198.
10. *I and Thou*, 97.
11. "The Hidden Light," in Martin Buber, *Or Haganuz* (Tel Aviv: Schocken Publishing House, 1979), outside back cover.
12. "The Streets of Nehardea," in *Later Masters*, 50.
13. *I and Thou*, 82.
14. *I and Thou*, 83.
15. "With One Look," in *Early Masters*, 298.

Epilogue

1. *I and Thou*, 101.

FURTHER READING

Anderson, Rob, and Kenneth H. Cissna. *The Martin Buber–Carl Rogers Dialogue: A New Transcript with Commentary*. Albany, N.Y.: State University of New York Press, 1997. A carefully and richly annotated transcript of the 1957 dialogue between Martin Buber and Carl Rogers, the leading figure of client-centered psychotherapy.

Buber, Martin. *I and Thou*. Translated by Walter Kaufmann. New York: Touchstone, 1996.

———. *I and Thou*. Translated by Ronald Gregor Smith. New York: Scribner Classics, 2000. I find Smith's translation easier to follow.

———. *Tales of the Hasidim: Early Masters* and *Late Masters*. Translated by Olga Marx. New York: Schocken Books, 1975. Buber's anthology of Hasidic stories.

Friedman, Maurice. *The Life and Work of Martin Buber, The Early Years, The Middle Years* and *The Later Years*. New York: E. P. Dutton, 1981–1983. The encyclopedic, lucid, and loving three-volume biography and teachings written by Buber's foremost disciple and authority.

———. *Martin Buber: The Life of Dialogue*. New York: Routledge, 2002. Comprehensive and well organized, an erudite presentation of Buber's thought.

———, ed. *Meetings*. LaSalle, Il.: Open Court Publishing Company, 1975. Buber's fragmentary autobiographical writings.

Green, Arthur, and Barry W. Holtz. *Your Word Is Fire: The Hasidic Masters on Contemplative Prayer*. Woodstock, Vt.: Jewish Lights Publishing, 1993.

Hodes, Aubrey. *Martin Buber: An Intimate Portrait*. New York: Viking Press, 1971. A personal account of discussions with Buber woven with a summary of his thought.

Notes

Notes

About JEWISH LIGHTS Publishing

People of all faiths and backgrounds yearn for books that attract, engage, educate, and spiritually inspire.

Our principal goal is to stimulate thought and help all people learn about who the Jewish People are, where they come from, and what the future can be made to hold. While people of our diverse Jewish heritage are the primary audience, our books speak to people in the Christian world as well and will broaden their understanding of Judaism and the roots of their own faith.

We bring to you authors who are at the forefront of spiritual thought and experience. While each has something different to say, they all say it in a voice that you can hear.

Our books are designed to welcome you and then to engage, stimulate, and inspire. We judge our success not only by whether or not our books are beautiful and commercially successful, but by whether or not they make a difference in your life.

We at Jewish Lights take great care to produce beautiful books that present meaningful spiritual content in a form that reflects the art of making high quality books. Therefore, we want to acknowledge those who contributed to the production of this book.

Stuart M. Matlins

Stuart M. Matlins, Publisher

PRODUCTION
Sara Dismukes, Tim Holtz,
Martha McKinney & Bridgett Taylor

EDITORIAL
Rebecca Castellano, Amanda Dupuis, Polly Short Mahoney,
Lauren Seidman & Emily Wichland

COVER & TEXT DESIGN
Bridgett Taylor

TYPESETTING
Bridgett Taylor

COVER / TEXT PRINTING & BINDING
Versa Press, East Peoria, Illinois

Spirituality/Jewish Meditation

Aleph-Bet Yoga
Embodying the Hebrew Letters for Physical and Spiritual Well-Being
by *Steven A. Rapp;* Foreword by *Tamar Frankiel* & *Judy Greenfeld;* Preface by *Hart Lazer*

Blends aspects of hatha yoga and the shapes of the Hebrew letters. Connects yoga practice with Jewish spiritual life. Easy-to-follow instructions, b/w photos.

7 x 10, 128 pp, Quality PB, b/w photos, ISBN 1-58023-162-4 **$16.95**

The Rituals & Practices of a Jewish Life
A Handbook for Personal Spiritual Renewal
by *Rabbi Kerry M. Olitzky* and *Rabbi Daniel Judson;* Foreword by *Vanessa L. Ochs;* Illustrated by *Joel Moskowitz*

This easy-to-use handbook explains the why, what, and how of ten specific areas of Jewish ritual and practice: morning and evening blessings, covering the head, blessings throughout the day, daily prayer, tefillin, tallit and *tallit katan,* Torah study, kashrut, *mikvah,* and entering Shabbat.

6 x 9, 272 pp, Quality PB, Illus., ISBN 1-58023-169-1 **$18.95**

Discovering Jewish Meditation: *Instruction & Guidance for Learning an Ancient Spiritual Practice* by Nan Fink Gefen 6 x 9, 208 pp, Quality PB, ISBN 1-58023-067-9 **$16.95**

The Handbook of Jewish Meditation Practices: *A Guide for Enriching the Sabbath and Other Days of Your Life* by Rabbi David A. Cooper
6 x 9, 208 pp, Quality PB, ISBN 1-58023-102-0 **$16.95**

Meditation from the Heart of Judaism: *Today's Teachers Share Their Practices, Techniques, and Faith* Ed. by Avram Davis 6 x 9, 256 pp, Quality PB, ISBN 1-58023-049-0 **$16.95**

The Way of Flame: *A Guide to the Forgotten Mystical Tradition of Jewish Meditation* by Avram Davis 4½ x 8, 176 pp, Quality PB, ISBN 1-58023-060-1 **$15.95**

Minding the Temple of the Soul: *Balancing Body, Mind, and Spirit through Traditional Jewish Prayer, Movement, and Meditation* by Tamar Frankiel and Judy Greenfeld
7 x 10, 184 pp, Quality PB, Illus., ISBN 1-879045-64-8 **$16.95**

Entering the Temple of Dreams: *Jewish Prayers, Movements, and Meditations for the End of the Day* by Tamar Frankiel and Judy Greenfeld
7 x 10, 192 pp, Illus., Quality PB, ISBN 1-58023-079-2 **$16.95**

The Way Into... Series

A major multi-volume series to be completed over the next several years, *The Way Into...* **provides an accessible and usable "guided tour" of the Jewish faith, its people, its history and beliefs—in total, an introduction to Judaism for adults that will enable them to understand and interact with sacred texts.**

Each volume is written by a major modern scholar and teacher, and is organized around an important concept of Judaism.

The Way Into... will enable all readers to achieve a real sense of Jewish cultural literacy through guided study. Available volumes:

The Way Into Torah
by *Dr. Norman J. Cohen*

What is "Torah"? What are the different approaches to studying Torah? What are the different levels of understanding Torah? For whom is study intended? Explores the origins and development of Torah, why it should be studied and how to do it. An easy-to-use, easy-to-understand introduction to an ancient subject.
6 x 9, 176 pp, HC, ISBN 1-58023-028-8 **$21.95**

The Way Into Jewish Prayer
by *Dr. Lawrence A. Hoffman*

Explores the reasons for and the ways of Jewish prayer. Opens the door to 3,000 years of the Jewish way to God by making available all you need to feel at home in Jewish worship. Provides basic definitions of the terms you need to know as well as thoughtful analysis of the depth that lies beneath Jewish prayer.
6 x 9, 224 pp, HC, ISBN 1-58023-027-X **$21.95**

The Way Into Encountering God in Judaism
by *Dr. Neil Gillman*

Explains how Jews have encountered God throughout history—and today—by exploring the many metaphors for God in Jewish tradition. Explores the Jewish tradition's passionate but also conflicting ways of relating to God as Creator, relational partner, and a force in history and nature.
6 x 9, 240 pp, HC, ISBN 1-58023-025-3 **$21.95**

The Way Into Jewish Mystical Tradition
by *Rabbi Lawrence Kushner*

Explains the principles of Jewish mystical thinking, their religious and spiritual significance, and how they relate to our lives. A book that allows us to experience and understand the Jewish mystical approach to our place in the world.
6 x 9, 224 pp, HC, ISBN 1-58023-029-6 **$21.95**

Theology/Philosophy

Love and Terror in the God Encounter
The Theological Legacy of Rabbi Joseph B. Soloveitchik
by *Dr. David Hartman*

Renowned scholar David Hartman explores the sometimes surprising intersection of Soloveitchik's rootedness in halakhic tradition with his genuine responsiveness to modern Western theology. An engaging look at one of the most important Jewish thinkers of the twentieth century.
6 x 9, 240 pp, Quality PB, ISBN 1-58023-176-4 **$19.95**; HC, ISBN 1-58023-112-8 **$25.00**

These Are the Words: *A Vocabulary of Jewish Spiritual Life*
by *Arthur Green*

What are the most essential ideas, concepts and terms that an educated person needs to know about Judaism? From *Adonai* (My Lord) to *zekhut* (merit), this enlightening and entertaining journey through Judaism teaches us the 149 core Hebrew words that constitute the basic vocabulary of Jewish spiritual life. 6 x 9, 304 pp, Quality PB, ISBN 1-58023-107-1 **$18.95**

Broken Tablets: *Restoring the Ten Commandments and Ourselves*
Ed. by *Rabbi Rachel S. Mikva*; Intro. by *Rabbi Lawrence Kushner*   AWARD WINNER!

Twelve outstanding spiritual leaders each share profound and personal thoughts about these biblical commands and why they have such a special hold on us.
6 x 9, 192 pp, Quality PB, ISBN 1-58023-158-6 **$16.95**; HC, ISBN 1-58023-066-0 **$21.95**

A Heart of Many Rooms: *Celebrating the Many Voices within Judaism* AWARD WINNER!
by Dr. David Hartman 6 x 9, 352 pp, Quality PB, ISBN 1-58023-156-X **$19.95**;
HC, ISBN 1-58023-048-2 **$24.95**

A Living Covenant: *The Innovative Spirit in Traditional Judaism* AWARD WINNER!
by Dr. David Hartman 6 x 9, 368 pp, Quality PB, ISBN 1-58023-011-3 **$18.95**

Evolving Halakhah: *A Progressive Approach to Traditional Jewish Law*
by Rabbi Dr. Moshe Zemer 6 x 9, 480 pp, Quality PB, ISBN 1-58023-127-6 **$29.95**;
HC, ISBN 1-58023-002-4 **$40.00**

The Death of Death: *Resurrection and Immortality in Jewish Thought* AWARD WINNER!
by Dr. Neil Gillman 6 x 9, 336 pp, Quality PB, ISBN 1-58023-081-4 **$18.95**

The Last Trial: *On the Legends and Lore of the Command to Abraham to Offer Isaac as a Sacrifice* by Shalom Spiegel 6 x 9, 208 pp, Quality PB, ISBN 1-879045-29-X **$17.95**

Tormented Master: *The Life and Spiritual Quest of Rabbi Nahman of Bratslav*
by Dr. Arthur Green 6 x 9, 416 pp, Quality PB, ISBN 1-879045-11-7 **$18.95**

The Earth Is the Lord's: *The Inner World of the Jew in Eastern Europe*
by Abraham Joshua Heschel 5½ x 8, 128 pp, Quality PB, ISBN 1-879045-42-7 **$14.95**

A Passion for Truth: *Despair and Hope in Hasidism* by Abraham Joshua Heschel
5½ x 8, 352 pp, Quality PB, ISBN 1-879045-41-9 **$18.95**

Your Word Is Fire: *The Hasidic Masters on Contemplative Prayer* Ed. by Dr. Arthur Green and Dr. Barry W. Holtz 6 x 9, 160 pp, Quality PB, ISBN 1-879045-25-7 **$15.95**

Children's Spirituality

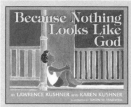

Because Nothing Looks Like God
by *Lawrence and Karen Kushner*
Full-color illus. by *Dawn W. Majewski*

For ages
4 & up

MULTICULTURAL, NONDENOMINATIONAL, NONSECTARIAN

What is God like? The first collaborative work by husband-and-wife team Lawrence and Karen Kushner introduces children to the possibilities of spiritual life. Real-life examples of happiness and sadness—from goodnight stories, to the hope and fear felt the first time at bat, to the closing moments of life—invite us to explore, together with our children, the questions we all have about God, no matter what our age.

11 x 8½, 32 pp, HC, Full-color illus., ISBN 1-58023-092-X **$16.95**

*Also available: **Teacher's Guide,** 8½ x 11, 22 pp, PB, ISBN 1-58023-140-3 **$6.95** For ages 5–8*

Where Is God?
What Does God Look Like?
How Does God Make Things Happen? (Board Books)

For ages
0–4

by *Lawrence and Karen Kushner*; Full-color illus. by *Dawn W. Majewski*

Gently invites children to become aware of God's presence all around them. Three board books abridged from *Because Nothing Looks Like God* by Lawrence and Karen Kushner.
Each 5 x 5, 24 pp, Board, Full-color illus. **$7.95** SKYLIGHT PATHS Books

Sharing Blessings
Children's Stories for Exploring the Spirit of the Jewish Holidays

For ages
6 & up

by *Rahel Musleah* and *Rabbi Michael Klayman*; Full-color illus.

What is the spiritual message of each of the Jewish holidays? How do we teach it to our children? Through stories about one family's life, *Sharing Blessings* explores ways to get into the *spirit* of thirteen different holidays.
8½ x 11, 64 pp, HC, Full-color illus., ISBN 1-879045-71-0 **$18.95**

The Book of Miracles   AWARD WINNER!
A Young Person's Guide to Jewish Spiritual Awareness

For ages
9 & up

by *Lawrence Kushner*

Introduces kids to a way of everyday spiritual thinking to last a lifetime. Kushner, whose award-winning books have brought spirituality to life for countless adults, now shows young people how to use Judaism as a foundation on which to build their lives.
6 x 9, 96 pp, HC, 2-color illus., ISBN 1-879045-78-8 **$16.95**

Children's Spirituality

In Our Image
God's First Creatures AWARD WINNER!

For ages 4 & up

by *Nancy Sohn Swartz*
Full-color illus. by *Melanie Hall*

A playful new twist on the Creation story—from the perspective of the animals. Celebrates the interconnectedness of nature and the harmony of all living things. "The vibrantly colored illustrations nearly leap off the page in this delightful interpretation." —*School Library Journal*
9 x 12, 32 pp, HC, Full-color illus., ISBN 1-879045-99-0 **$16.95**

God's Paintbrush AWARD WINNER!

For ages 4 & up

by *Sandy Eisenberg Sasso*; Full-color illus. by *Annette Compton*

Invites children of all faiths and backgrounds to encounter God openly in their own lives. Wonderfully interactive; provides questions adult and child can explore together at the end of each episode. 11 x 8½, 32 pp, HC, Full-color illus., ISBN 1-879045-22-2 **$16.95**

Also available: A Teacher's Guide: **A Guide for Jewish & Christian Educators and Parents**
8½ x 11, 32 pp, PB, ISBN 1-879045-57-5 **$8.95**

God's Paintbrush Celebration Kit 9½ x 12, HC, Includes 5 sessions/40 full-color Activity Sheets and Teacher Folder with complete instructions, ISBN 1-58023-050-4 **$21.95**

In God's Name AWARD WINNER!

For ages 4 & up

by *Sandy Eisenberg Sasso*; Full-color illus. by *Phoebe Stone*

Like an ancient myth in its poetic text and vibrant illustrations, this award-winning modern fable about the search for God's name celebrates the diversity and, at the same time, the unity of all people. 9 x 12, 32 pp, HC, Full-color illus., ISBN 1-879045-26-5 **$16.95**

What Is God's Name? (A Board Book)

For ages 0–4

An abridged board book version of award-winning *In God's Name.*
5 x 5, 24 pp, Board, Full-color illus., ISBN 1-893361-10-1 **$7.95** A SKYLIGHT PATHS Book

The 11th Commandment: *Wisdom from Our Children*

For all ages

by *The Children of America* AWARD WINNER!

"If there were an Eleventh Commandment, what would it be?" Children of many religious denominations across America answer this question—in their own drawings and words. "A rare book of spiritual celebration for all people, of all ages, for all time."—*Bookviews*
8 x 10, 48 pp, HC, Full-color illus., ISBN 1-879045-46-X **$16.95**

Children's Spirituality

Cain & Abel AWARD WINNER!
Finding the Fruits of Peace
by *Sandy Eisenberg Sasso*
Full-color illus. by *Joani Keller Rothenberg*

For ages 5 & up

A sensitive recasting of the ancient tale shows we have the power to deal with anger in positive ways. Provides questions for kids and adults to explore together. "Editor's Choice"—American Library Association's *Booklist*
9 x 12, 32 pp, HC, Full-color illus., ISBN 1-58023-123-3 **$16.95**

For Heaven's Sake AWARD WINNER!
by *Sandy Eisenberg Sasso*; Full-color illus. by *Kathryn Kunz Finney*

For ages 4 & up

Everyone talked about heaven, but no one would say what heaven was or how to find it. So Isaiah decides to find out. 9 x 12, 32 pp, HC, Full-color illus., ISBN 1-58023-054-7 **$16.95**

God Said Amen AWARD WINNER!
by *Sandy Eisenberg Sasso*; Full-color illus. by *Avi Katz*

For ages 4 & up

Inspiring tale of two kingdoms: one overflowing with water but without oil to light its lamps; the other blessed with oil but no water to grow its gardens. The kingdoms' rulers ask God for help but are too stubborn to ask each other. Shows that we need only reach out to each other to find God's answer to our prayers. 9 x 12, 32 pp, HC, Full-color illus., ISBN 1-58023-080-6 **$16.95**

God in Between AWARD WINNER!
by *Sandy Eisenberg Sasso*; Full-color illus. by *Sally Sweetland*

For ages 4 & up

If you wanted to find God, where would you look? This magical, mythical tale teaches that God can be found where we are: within all of us and the relationships between us.
9 x 12, 32 pp, HC, Full-color illus., ISBN 1-879045-86-9 **$16.95**

Noah's Wife: The Story of Naamah
by *Sandy Eisenberg Sasso*; Full-color illus. by *Bethanne Andersen* AWARD WINNER!

For ages 4 & up

Opens religious imaginations to new ideas about the story of the Flood. When God tells Noah to bring the animals onto the ark, God also calls on Naamah, Noah's wife, to save each plant on Earth. 9 x 12, 32 pp, HC, Full-color illus., ISBN 1-58023-134-9 **$16.95**

But God Remembered AWARD WINNER!
Stories of Women from Creation to the Promised Land
by *Sandy Eisenberg Sasso*; Full-color illus. by *Bethanne Andersen*

For ages 8 & up

Vibrantly brings to life four stories of courageous and strong women from ancient tradition; all teach important values through their actions and faith.
9 x 12, 32 pp, HC, Full-color illus., ISBN 1-879045-43-5 **$16.95**

Life Cycle/Grief/Divorce

Divorce Is a Mitzvah: *A Practical Guide to Finding Wholeness and Holiness When Your Marriage Dies*
by *Rabbi Perry Netter;*
Afterword—"Afterwards: New Jewish Divorce Rituals"—by *Rabbi Laura Geller*

What does Judaism tell you about divorce? This first-of-its-kind handbook provides practical wisdom from biblical and rabbinic teachings and modern psychological research, as well as information and strength from a Jewish perspective for those experiencing the challenging life-transition of divorce. 6 x 9, 224 pp, Quality PB, ISBN 1-58023-172-1 **$16.95**

Against the Dying of the Light
A Parent's Story of Love, Loss and Hope
by *Leonard Fein*

The sudden death of a child. A personal tragedy beyond description. Rage and despair deeper than sorrow. What can come from it? Raw wisdom and defiant hope. In this unusual exploration of heartbreak and healing, Fein chronicles the sudden death of his 30-year-old daughter and reveals what the progression of grief can teach each one of us.
5½ x 8½, 176 pp, HC, ISBN 1-58023-110-1 **$19.95**

Mourning & Mitzvah, 2nd Ed.: *A Guided Journal for Walking the Mourner's Path through Grief to Healing* with *Over 60 Guided Exercises*
by *Anne Brener, L.C.S.W.*

For those who mourn a death, for those who would help them, for those who face a loss of any kind, Brener teaches us the power and strength available to us in the fully experienced mourning process. Revised and expanded. 7½ x 9, 304 pp, Quality PB, ISBN 1-58023-113-6 **$19.95**

Grief in Our Seasons: *A Mourner's Kaddish Companion*
by *Rabbi Kerry M. Olitzky*

A wise and inspiring selection of sacred Jewish writings and a simple, powerful ancient ritual for mourners to read each day, to help hold the memory of their loved ones in their hearts. Offers a comforting, step-by-step daily link to saying Kaddish.
4½ x 6½, 448 pp, Quality PB, ISBN 1-879045-55-9 **$15.95**

Tears of Sorrow, Seeds of Hope
A Jewish Spiritual Companion for Infertility and Pregnancy Loss
by Rabbi Nina Beth Cardin   6 x 9, 192 pp, HC, ISBN 1-58023-017-2 **$19.95**

A Time to Mourn, A Time to Comfort
A Guide to Jewish Bereavement and Comfort
by Dr. Ron Wolfson 7 x 9, 336 pp, Quality PB, ISBN 1-879045-96-6 **$18.95**

When a Grandparent Dies
A Kid's Own Remembering Workbook for Dealing with Shiva and the Year Beyond
by Nechama Liss-Levinson, Ph.D.
8 x 10, 48 pp, HC, Illus., 2-color text, ISBN 1-879045-44-3 **$15.95**   **For ages 7–13**

Life Cycle & Holidays

The Jewish Family Fun Book: *Holiday Projects, Everyday Activities, and Travel Ideas with Jewish Themes*
by *Danielle Dardashti* & *Roni Sarig;* Illustrated by *Avi Katz*
With almost 100 easy-to-do activities to re-invigorate age-old Jewish customs and make them fun for the whole family, this complete sourcebook details activities for fun at home and away from home, including meaningful everyday and holiday crafts, recipes, travel guides, enriching entertainment and much, much more. Illustrated.
6 x 9, 288 pp, Quality PB, Illus., ISBN 1-58023-171-3 **$18.95**

The Book of Jewish Sacred Practices
CLAL's Guide to Everyday & Holiday Rituals & Blessings
Ed. by *Rabbi Irwin Kula* & *Vanessa L. Ochs, Ph.D.*
A meditation, blessing, profound Jewish teaching, and ritual for more than one hundred everyday events and holidays. 6 x 9, 368 pp, Quality PB, ISBN 1-58023-152-7 **$18.95**

Celebrating Your New Jewish Daughter: *Creating Jewish Ways to Welcome Baby Girls into the Covenant—New and Traditional Ceremonies*
by Debra Nussbaum Cohen; Foreword by Rabbi Sandy Eisenberg Sasso
6 x 9, 272 pp, Quality PB, ISBN 1-58023-090-3 **$18.95**

The New Jewish Baby Book AWARD WINNER!
Names, Ceremonies & Customs—A Guide for Today's Families
by Anita Diamant 6 x 9, 336 pp, Quality PB, ISBN 1-879045-28-1 **$18.95**

Parenting As a Spiritual Journey
Deepening Ordinary & Extraordinary Events into Sacred Occasions
by Rabbi Nancy Fuchs-Kreimer 6 x 9, 224 pp, Quality PB, ISBN 1-58023-016-4 **$16.95**

Putting God on the Guest List, 2nd Ed. AWARD WINNER!
How to Reclaim the Spiritual Meaning of Your Child's Bar or Bat Mitzvah
by Rabbi Jeffrey K. Salkin 6 x 9, 224 pp, Quality PB, ISBN 1-879045-59-1 **$16.95**

The Bar/Bat Mitzvah Memory Book: *An Album for Treasuring the Spiritual Celebration* by Rabbi Jeffrey K. Salkin and Nina Salkin
8 x 10, 48 pp, Deluxe HC, 2-color text, ribbon marker, ISBN 1-58023-111-X **$19.95**

For Kids—Putting God on Your Guest List
How to Claim the Spiritual Meaning of Your Bar or Bat Mitzvah
by Rabbi Jeffrey K. Salkin 6 x 9, 144 pp, Quality PB, ISBN 1-58023-015-6 **$14.95**

Bar/Bat Mitzvah Basics, 2nd Ed.: *A Practical Family Guide to Coming of Age Together*
Ed. by Cantor Helen Leneman 6 x 9, 240 pp, Quality PB, ISBN 1-58023-151-9 **$18.95**

Hanukkah, 2nd Ed.: *The Family Guide to Spiritual Celebration*—The Art of Jewish Living
by Dr. Ron Wolfson 7 x 9, 240 pp, Quality PB, Illus., ISBN 1-58023-122-5 **$18.95**

Shabbat, 2nd Ed.: *Preparing for and Celebrating the Sabbath*—The Art of Jewish Living
by Dr. Ron Wolfson 7 x 9, 320 pp, Quality PB, Illus., ISBN 1-58023-164-0 **$19.95**

Passover, 2nd Ed.: *The Family Guide to Spiritual Celebration*—The Art of Jewish Living
by Dr. Ron Wolfson 7 x 9, 352 pp, Quality PB, ISBN 1-58023-174-8 **$19.95**

Healing/Wellness/Recovery

Jewish Paths toward Healing and Wholeness
A Personal Guide to Dealing with Suffering
by *Rabbi Kerry M. Olitzky*; Foreword by *Debbie Friedman*

Why me? Why do we suffer? How can we heal? Grounded in personal experience with illness and Jewish spiritual traditions, this book provides healing rituals, psalms and prayers that help readers initiate a dialogue with God, to guide them along the complicated path of healing and wholeness. 6 x 9, 192 pp, Quality PB, ISBN 1-58023-068-7 **$15.95**

Healing of Soul, Healing of Body
Spiritual Leaders Unfold the Strength & Solace in Psalms
Ed. by *Rabbi Simkha Y. Weintraub, CSW,* for The National Center for Jewish Healing

For those who are facing illness and those who care for them. Inspiring commentaries on ten psalms for healing by eminent spiritual leaders reflecting all Jewish movements make the power of the psalms accessible to all.

6 x 9, 128 pp, Quality PB, Illus., 2-color text, ISBN 1-879045-31-1 **$14.95**

Jewish Pastoral Care
A Practical Handbook from Traditional and Contemporary Sources
Ed. by *Rabbi Dayle A. Friedman*

Gives today's Jewish pastoral counselors practical guidelines based in the Jewish tradition.
6 x 9, 464 pp, HC, ISBN 1-58023-078-4 **$35.00**

Twelve Jewish Steps to Recovery: *A Personal Guide to Turning from Alcoholism & Other Addictions—Drugs, Food, Gambling, Sex . . .* by Rabbi Kerry M. Olitzky & Stuart A. Copans, M.D. Preface by Abraham J. Twerski, M.D.; "Getting Help" by JACS Foundation 6 x 9, 144 pp, Quality PB, ISBN 1-879045-09-5 **$14.95**

One Hundred Blessings Every Day: *Daily Twelve Step Recovery Affirmations, Exercises for Personal Growth & Renewal Reflecting Seasons of the Jewish Year* by Rabbi Kerry M. Olitzky 4½ x 6½, 432 pp, Quality PB, ISBN 1-879045-30-3 **$14.95**

Recovery from Codependence: *A Jewish Twelve Steps Guide to Healing Your Soul* by Rabbi Kerry M. Olitzky 6 x 9, 160 pp, Quality PB, ISBN 1-879045-32-X **$13.95**

Renewed Each Day: *Daily Twelve Step Recovery Meditations Based on the Bible* by Rabbi Kerry M. Olitzky & Aaron Z. *Vol. I: Genesis & Exodus; Vol. II: Leviticus, Numbers and Deuteronomy*
Vol. I: 6 x 9, 224 pp, Quality PB, ISBN 1-879045-12-5 **$14.95**
Vol. II: 6 x 9, 280 pp, Quality PB, ISBN 1-879045-13-3 **$14.95**

Spirituality

My People's Prayer Book: *Traditional Prayers, Modern Commentaries*
Ed. by *Dr. Lawrence A. Hoffman*

Provides a diverse and exciting commentary to the traditional liturgy, helping modern men and women find new wisdom in Jewish prayer, and bring liturgy into their lives. Each book includes Hebrew text, modern translation, and commentaries *from all perspectives* of the Jewish world.

Vol. 1—*The Sh'ma and Its Blessings*, 7 x 10, 168 pp, HC, ISBN 1-879045-79-6 **$23.95**
Vol. 2—*The Amidah*, 7 x 10, 240 pp, HC, ISBN 1-879045-80-X **$23.95**
Vol. 3—*P'sukei D'zimrah* (Morning Psalms), 7 x 10, 240 pp, HC, ISBN 1-879045-81-8 **$24.95**
Vol. 4—*Seder K'riat Hatorah* (The Torah Service), 7 x 10, 264 pp, HC, ISBN 1-879045-82-6 **$23.95**
Vol. 5—*Birkhot Hashachar* (Morning Blessings), 7 x 10, 240 pp, HC, ISBN 1-879045-83-4 **$24.95**
Vol. 6—*Tachanun and Concluding Prayers*, 7 x 10, 240 pp, HC, ISBN 1-879045-84-2 **$24.95**

Six Jewish Spiritual Paths: *A Rationalist Looks at Spirituality*
by Rabbi Rifat Sonsino
6 x 9, 208 pp, Quality PB, ISBN 1-58023-167-5 **$16.95**; HC, ISBN 1-58023-095-4 **$21.95**

Becoming a Congregation of Learners
Learning as a Key to Revitalizing Congregational Life by Isa Aron, Ph.D.;
Foreword by Rabbi Lawrence A. Hoffman, Co-Developer, Synagogue 2000
6 x 9, 304 pp, Quality PB, ISBN 1-58023-089-X **$19.95**

Self, Struggle & Change
Family Conflict Stories in Genesis and Their Healing Insights for Our Lives
by Dr. Norman J. Cohen 6 x 9, 224 pp, Quality PB, ISBN 1-879045-66-4 **$16.95**

Voices from Genesis: *Guiding Us through the Stages of Life*
by Dr. Norman J. Cohen 6 x 9, 192 pp, Quality PB, ISBN 1-58023-118-7 **$16.95**

Ancient Secrets: *Using the Stories of the Bible to Improve Our Everyday Lives*
by Rabbi Levi Meier, Ph.D. 5½ x 8½, 288 pp, Quality PB, ISBN 1-58023-064-4 **$16.95**

The Business Bible: *10 New Commandments for Bringing Spirituality & Ethical Values into the Workplace*
by Rabbi Wayne Dosick 5½ x 8½, 208 pp, Quality PB, ISBN 1-58023-101-2 **$14.95**

Being God's Partner: *How to Find the Hidden Link Between Spirituality and Your Work*
by Rabbi Jeffrey K. Salkin; Intro. by Norman Lear **AWARD WINNER!**
6 x 9, 192 pp, Quality PB, ISBN 1-879045-65-6 **$17.95**; HC, ISBN 1-879045-37-0 **$19.95**

God & the Big Bang
Discovering Harmony Between Science & Spirituality **AWARD WINNER!**
by Daniel C. Matt 6 x 9, 224 pp, Quality PB, ISBN 1-879045-89-3 **$16.95**

Soul Judaism: *Dancing with God into a New Era*
by Rabbi Wayne Dosick 5½ x 8½, 304 pp, Quality PB, ISBN 1-58023-053-9 **$16.95**

Finding Joy: *A Practical Spiritual Guide to Happiness* **AWARD WINNER!**
by Rabbi Dannel I. Schwartz with Mark Hass
6 x 9, 192 pp, Quality PB, ISBN 1-58023-009-1 **$14.95**; HC, ISBN 1-879045-53-2 **$19.95**

Spirituality—The Kushner Series
Books by Lawrence Kushner

The Way Into Jewish Mystical Tradition

Explains the principles of Jewish mystical thinking, their religious and spiritual significance, and how they relate to our lives. A book that allows us to experience and understand the Jewish mystical approach to our place in the world.
6 x 9, 224 pp, HC, ISBN 1-58023-029-6 **$21.95**

Jewish Spirituality: *A Brief Introduction for Christians*

Addresses Christian's questions, revealing the essence of Judaism in a way that people whose own tradition traces its roots to Judaism can understand and appreciate.
5½ x 8½, 112 pp, Quality PB, ISBN 1-58023-150-0 **$12.95**

Eyes Remade for Wonder: *The Way of Jewish Mysticism and Sacred Living*
A Lawrence Kushner Reader Intro. by *Thomas Moore*

Whether you are new to Kushner or a devoted fan, you'll find inspiration here. With samplings from each of Kushner's works, and a generous amount of new material, this book is to be read and reread, each time discovering deeper layers of meaning in our lives.
6 x 9, 240 pp, Quality PB, ISBN 1-58023-042-3 **$18.95**; HC, ISBN 1-58023-014-8 **$23.95**

Invisible Lines of Connection: *Sacred Stories of the Ordinary* AWARD WINNER!
5½ x 8½, 160 pp, Quality PB, ISBN 1-879045-98-2 **$15.95**

Honey from the Rock: *An Introduction to Jewish Mysticism* SPECIAL ANNIVERSARY EDITION
6 x 9, 176 pp, Quality PB, ISBN 1-58023-073-3 **$15.95**

The Book of Letters: *A Mystical Hebrew Alphabet* AWARD WINNER!
Popular HC Edition, 6 x 9, 80 pp, 2-color text, ISBN 1-879045-00-1 **$24.95**; *Deluxe Gift Edition*, 9 x 12, 80 pp, HC, 4-color text, ornamentation, slipcase, ISBN 1-879045-01-X **$79.95**; *Collector's Limited Edition*, 9 x 12, 80 pp, HC, gold-embossed pages, hand-assembled slipcase. With silkscreened print. Limited to 500 signed and numbered copies, ISBN 1-879045-04-4 **$349.00**

The Book of Words: *Talking Spiritual Life, Living Spiritual Talk* AWARD WINNER!
6 x 9, 160 pp, Quality PB, 2-color text, ISBN 1-58023-020-2 **$16.95**; HC, ISBN 1-879045-35-4 **$21.95**

God Was in This Place & I, i Did Not Know: *Finding Self, Spirituality and Ultimate Meaning*
6 x 9, 192 pp, Quality PB, ISBN 1-879045-33-8 **$16.95**

The River of Light: *Jewish Mystical Awareness* SPECIAL ANNIVERSARY EDITION
6 x 9, 192 pp, Quality PB, ISBN 1-58023-096-2 **$16.95**

Because Nothing Looks Like God
by Lawrence and Karen Kushner; Full-color illus. by Dawn W. Majewski
11 x 8½, 32 pp, HC, Full-color illus., ISBN 1-58023-092-X **$16.95** For ages 4 & up

Spirituality & More

The Jewish Lights Spirituality Handbook
A Guide to Understanding, Exploring & Living a Spiritual Life
Ed. by *Stuart M. Matlins, Editor in Chief, Jewish Lights Publishing*

Rich, creative material from over fifty spiritual leaders on every aspect of Jewish spirituality today: prayer, meditation, mysticism, study, rituals, special days, the everyday, and more.
6 x 9, 456 pp, Quality PB, ISBN 1-58023-093-8 **$18.95**; HC, ISBN 1-58023-100-4 **$24.95**

The Story of the Jews: *A 4,000-Year Adventure—A Graphic History Book*
Written and illustrated by *Stan Mack*

Through witty cartoons and accurate narrative, illustrates the major characters and events that have shaped the Jewish people and culture. For all ages.
6 x 9, 304 pp, Quality PB, Illus., ISBN 1-58023-155-1 **$16.95**

The Jewish Prophet: *Visionary Words from Moses and Miriam to Henrietta Szold and A. J. Heschel*
by *Rabbi Dr. Michael J. Shire*

This beautifully illustrated collection of Jewish prophecy features the lives and teachings of thirty men and women, from biblical times to modern day. Provides an inspiring and informative description of the role each played in their own time, and an explanation of why we should know about them in our time. Illustrated with illuminations from medieval Hebrew manuscripts.
6½ x 8½, 128 pp, HC, 123 full-color illus., ISBN 1-58023-168-3 **$25.00**

The Enneagram and Kabbalah: *Reading Your Soul*
by Rabbi Howard A. Addison 6 x 9, 176 pp, Quality PB, ISBN 1-58023-001-6 **$15.95**

Cast in God's Image: *Discover Your Personality Type Using the Enneagram and Kabbalah*
by Rabbi Howard A. Addison 7 x 9, 176 pp, Quality PB, ISBN 1-58023-124-1 **$16.95**

Mystery Midrash: *An Anthology of Jewish Mystery & Detective Fiction* AWARD WINNER!
Ed. by Lawrence W. Raphael 6 x 9, 304 pp, Quality PB, ISBN 1-58023-055-5 **$16.95**

Criminal Kabbalah: *An Intriguing Anthology of Jewish Mystery & Detective Fiction*
Ed. by Lawrence W. Raphael; Foreword by Laurie R. King
6 x 9, 256 pp, Quality PB, ISBN 1-58023-109-8 **$16.95**

Sacred Intentions: *Daily Inspiration to Strengthen the Spirit, Based on Jewish Wisdom*
by Rabbi Kerry M. Olitzky & Rabbi Lori Forman
4½ x 6½, 448 pp, Quality PB, ISBN 1-58023-061-X **$15.95**

Restful Reflections: *Nighttime Inspiration to Calm the Soul, Based on Jewish Wisdom*
by Rabbi Kerry M. Olitzky & Rabbi Lori Forman
4½ x 6½, 448 pp, Quality PB, ISBN 1-58023-091-1 **$15.95**

Embracing the Covenant: *Converts to Judaism Talk About Why & How* Ed. by Rabbi Allan Berkowitz & Patti Moskovitz 6 x 9, 192 pp, Quality PB, ISBN 1-879045-50-8 **$16.95**

Wandering Stars: *An Anthology of Jewish Fantasy & Science Fiction* Ed. by Jack Dann; Intro. by Isaac Asimov 6 x 9, 272 pp, Quality PB, ISBN 1-58023-005-9 **$16.95**

Israel—A Spiritual Travel Guide: *A Companion for the Modern Jewish Pilgrim* AWARD WINNER!
by Rabbi Lawrence A. Hoffman 4¾ x 10, 256 pp, Quality PB, ISBN 1-879045-56-7 **$18.95**